THE CANAANITES

CASCADE COMPANIONS

The Christian theological tradition provides an embarrassment of riches: from Scripture to modern scholarship, we are blessed with a vast and complex theological inheritance. And yet this feast of traditional riches is too frequently inaccessible to the general reader.

The Cascade Companions series addresses the challenge by publishing books that combine academic rigor with broad appeal and readability. They aim to introduce nonspecialist readers to that vital storehouse of authors, documents, themes, histories, arguments, and movements that comprise this heritage with brief yet compelling volumes.

RECENT TITLES IN THIS SERIES:

THE CANAANITES

*Their History and Culture
from Texts and Artifacts*

MARY ELLEN BUCK

CASCADE *Books* • Eugene, Oregon

THE CANAANITES
Their History and Culture from Texts and Artifacts

Cascade Companions

Cascade Books
An Imprint of Wipf and Stock Publishers
199 W. 8th Ave., Suite 3
Eugene, OR 97401

www.wipfandstock.com

PAPERBACK ISBN: 978-1-5326-1804-8
HARDCOVER ISBN: 978-1-4982-4325-4
EBOOK ISBN: 978-1-4982-4324-7

Cataloguing-in-Publication data:

Names: Buck, Mary Ellen, author

Title: The Canaanites : their history and culture from texts and artefacts / Mary Ellen Buck.

Description: Eugene, OR: Cascade Books, 2019 | Series: Cascade Companions | Includes bibliographical references.

Identifiers: ISBN 978-1-5326-1804-8 (paperback) | ISBN 978-1-4982-4325-4 (hardcover) | ISBN 978-1-4982-4324-7 (ebook)

Subjects: LCSH: Canaanites—History | Canaanites—Historiography | Canaanites—Antiquities | Bronze age—Palestine | Excavations (Archaeology)—Palestine | Palestine—History—To 70A.D. | Bible—Old Testament—History and criticism

Classification: DS121.4 B83 2019 (paperback) | DS121.4 (ebook)

CONTENTS

FIGURES

Figures

CHRONOLOGY

This volume traces the history of the Canaanites back some five millennia to the Early Bronze Age in the Levant. Since textual sources are unavailable for much of this history, the archaeological periodization of the southern Levant has been used as a way to frame the chronological development of the Canaanites.

Date (Years BCE)	Archaeological Period	Abb.
3200 to 2500	Early Bronze Age II	EB II
2500 to 2200	Early Bronze Age III	EB III
2200 to 1800	Early Bronze Age IV (Middle Bronze I / Intermediate Bronze)	EB IV MB I / IB
1800 to 1550	Middle Bronze Age	MB
1550 to 1200	Late Bronze Age	LB
1200 to 950	Iron Age I	Iron I
950 to 586	Iron Age II–III	Iron II–III

ABBREVIATIONS

AF	*Altorientalische Forschungen*
AFO	*Archiv für Orientforschung*
ANES	*Ancient Near Eastern Studies*
BASOR	*Bulletin of the American Schools of Oriental Research*
EA	el–Amarna
EB/EBA	Early Bronze Age
GN	geographic name
IB/IBA	Intermediate Bronze Age
JAOS	*Journal of the American Oriental Society*
JNES	*Journal of Near Eastern Studies*
JS	*Journal of Semitics*
JSS	*Journal of Semitic Studies*
KTU	*Die keilalphabetischen Texte aus Ugarit, Ras Ibn Hani und anderen Orten*
LB/LBA	Late Bronze Age
MB/MBA	Middle Bronze Age
OB	Old Babylonian
Phoen.	Phoenician
RS	Ras Shamra
RSO	Ras Shamra–Ougarit
UF	Ugarit–Forschungen

1

CANAAN AND THE CANAANITES

"We are the descendants of the Canaanites that lived in the land of Palestine 5,000 years ago and continuously remained there to this day."
—Palestinian Authority Leader Mahmoud Abbas to the United Nations (February 2018)

"And after this, Avraham buried Sara his wife in the cave of the field of Machpelah . . . in the land of Canaan."
—Israeli Prime Minister Benjamin Netanyahu quoting Genesis 23:10 at the start of a cabinet meeting (July 2017)

1.1 INTRODUCTION

MODERN POLITICIANS OF THE Middle East leverage the terms "Canaan" and "Canaanite" as part of their political

1

discourse, indicating the immense impact that ancient history can have on the formation and expression of culture. The term "Canaanite" will be familiar to anyone who has even the most casual familiarity with the Hebrew Bible or Old Testament. The Canaanites feature prominently in the historical narratives of the Hebrew Bible, primarily in the texts of the Pentateuch and Joshua and Judges. Outside of the terminology for Israel itself, the term "Canaanite" is the most common ethnic descriptor found in the Hebrew Bible, occurring over 150 times, as well as three times in the New Testament, indicating its pervasive importance for the biblical narratives.[1] The land of Canaan is regularly seen as the promised allotment of Abraham and his descendants, beginning when Abraham is called to journey from Ur of the Chaldeans to the land of Canaan in Genesis 11:31 and 12:5–6. Thus, the Canaanites are regularly positioned as the foil of the nation of Israel, until the partial displacement of the Canaanites from the land of Canaan under Joshua (Josh 17:18).

With such prominent positioning in the narratives of the Hebrew Bible as well as the political narratives of the modern Middle East, it is important to gain a more complete and historically accurate perspective of the Canaanites, their land, history, and rich cultural heritage.

So, who were the Canaanites? Where did they live? What did they believe? What do we know about their culture and history? And why do they feature so prominently in the biblical narrative?

Before delving into these questions, let us begin our investigation by examining the meaning of the terms "Canaan" and "Canaanite."

---

1. Dever, *Who Were the Early Israelites and Where Did They Come From?* 219.

1.2 WHO WERE THE CANAANITES?

There is some debate regarding the meaning of the terms "Canaan" and "Canaanite." Michael Astour has claimed that the term "Canaan" goes back to a Northwest Semitic root (the Northwest Semitic language family includes languages such as Hebrew and Aramaic) *knʿ* meaning "to be low," referring perhaps to the lowlands or the land of the lowering sun on the western horizon of the Levant.[2] Others, such as Itamar Singer, disagree, suggesting that the term "Canaan" derives from a Hurrian term *kinaḫḫu* meaning "purple" or "red," referring to the beautiful purple-dyed cloth produced on the Phoenician coastland.[3]

Regardless of which interpretation should be accepted, it is clear that the term "Canaan" referred to the land along the coast of the Southern Levant, an area occupied today by Syria, Israel, Palestine, and Jordan. The term "Canaanite" therefore was used to refer to any individual or population residing in this region, beginning as early as the start of the Middle Bronze Age (ca. 1800 BCE) until the final appearance of this term in the Roman period (ca. 400 CE). This means that as populations migrated into the region, though they may have retained their unique ethnic identities and cultures, they were often recognized by outside populations as "Canaanites" or residents of the land of "Canaan." The benefit of applying this loose definition to the term "Canaanite" is the flexibility that this term allows as we trace their history back several thousand years in a single region. While the Canaanites from the third millennium were undoubtedly quite different from those in the first millennium, they shared one thing in common—their homeland.

2. Astour, "The Origin of the Terms 'Canaan', 'Phoenician', and 'Purple.'"

3. Singer, "Purple-Dyers in Lazpa," 36, n. 71.

1.3 THE LAND OF CANAAN

In the ancient world, life could only be supported by proximity to water and the ability to produce food for the population. Since much of the Middle East is arid desert, with little water, only certain territories could support life. In Mesopotamia, life was sustained by the Tigris and Euphrates Rivers, and irrigation was used to bring river water to farms. In the Levant, the area along the Mediterranean coast, life was sustained by regular rainfall, which allowed for dry farming to occur. The map below features this area of the Fertile Crescent where the presence of water and arable land supported life in the ancient world.

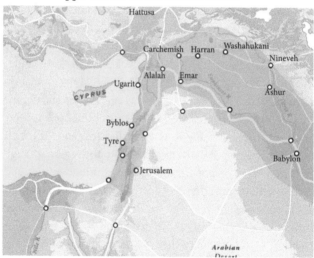

Figure 1.1: The Fertile Crescent
Map created by Dillon Paige

The land of Canaan, roughly corresponding to the area of the Southern Levant, covered the southwestern strip of the Fertile Crescent, occupying the territory of modern-day Lebanon, Jordan, Israel, and Palestine. We learn about the borders of the land of Canaan from numerous ancient sources including texts from Mari, Ugarit, Alalaḫ, and Amarna, but we glean the most detail from an Egyptian source from the late Nineteenth Dynasty, the Papyrus Anastasi I (ca. 1292 to 1189 BCE).[4] This text describes the region of Canaan in great detail, beginning at the coast of Lebanon, extending beyond Joppa to the "end of the land of Canaan," even to the city of Gaza. It shows that in the ancient Middle East, the territory of Canaan extended from the Lebanon and Anti-Lebanon mountain ranges in the north, to the Negev desert to the south. From east to west, the land of Canaan was bordered by the natural boundaries of the Ard as-Sawwan Desert in modern-day Jordan and the Mediterranean Sea. The territory of ancient Canaan is demarked below in Figure 1.2.

4. Wente, *Letters from Ancient Egypt*, 98–110. Wente dates the text to the second half of the nineteenth dynasty (1292 to 1189 BCE), roughly to the end of the Late Bronze Age.

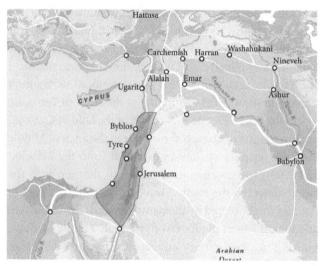

Figure 1.2: The Land of Canaan
Map created by Dillon Paige

The northern portion of the land of Canaan, also sometimes referred to as the Phoenician coast, was divided by large mountains and low-lying fertile valleys. These "mountainous promontories, which break up the region, hampered sea traffic, making certain areas independent of others. The territorial division is accentuated by a series of rivers that come down from the mountains and flow into the sea. In these areas the land is fertile, agriculture flourishes, and mountain timber is an important resource."[5] Over the course of history, in each of these fertile valleys relatively autonomous city-states flourished and maintained autonomous control.

To the south of the Phoenician coast, the area of modern-day Israel and Palestine, the land was divided into three main north/south topographical divisions: the coastal

5. Moscati, *The Phoenicians*, 26.

plain, the Shephelah (lowlands), and the hill country. The coastal plain was a flat, fertile area that supported farming and also allowed for easy passage for the purposes of trade and migration. The Shephelah marks the transition from the coastal plain to the higher hill country and is made up of a series of valleys and low-lying hills. Historically this area would also have been heavily farmed, but its valleys and hills hindered traffic through the region, and would also serve as a barrier to the interior of the land of Canaan. The hill country is marked by rugged and often impassable mountains, which could only be farmed if terraced.

To the east of the hill country, the mountains slope sharply down into the Jordan Valley, which hosts the lowest point on earth, the Dead Sea. The environs of this region are harsh, with high temperatures, though date palms can be supported in this region. This Jordan Valley once again slopes upward to the Jordanian highlands, which house important sites such as Petra. Further to the east and to the south, one encounters desert in which it is difficult to support life. Figure 1.3 below provides a close-up view of the land of Canaan, showcasing the various topographical features that constricted human settlement and trade.

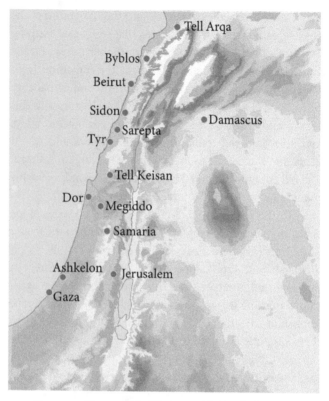

Figure 1.3: Topographical features of the Land of Canaan
Map created by Dillon Paige

With the Mediterranean Sea to the west and the arid desert regions of the Transjordan to the east, the only way to pass between regions in the ancient world was through the land of Canaan. Indeed, the territory of Canaan has been described as the "land between" as it served as the main connection point between Egypt in the south and the other major empires of the north, including Ugarit, Hatti, Babylon, and Assyria. Two main highways, the King's Highway and the Via Maris, or Way of the Sea, allowed messengers, armies, and migrating populations to pass through, making it the main link between empires. As the primary highway between regions, populations regularly migrated to, from, and through the region.

In addition to the presence of important highways, Canaan's long coastline provides access to ports and shipping traffic. Key port cities such as Joppa, Tyre, and Byblos were stopping points for ships journeying between Egypt, Anatolia, and the Aegean region to the west. Major cities developed over time to control trade along the land routes as well. Cities such as Megiddo, Hazor, and Damascus were strategically placed to control trade routes. The famous Silk Route also passed through Canaan, using cities such as Damascus and Tyre as key trade hubs for transporting luxury goods from the east to buyers in the Mediterranean region.

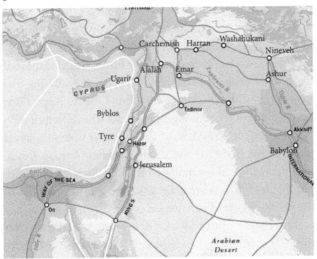

Figure 1.4: Map of trade routes in the ancient Middle East
Map created by Dillon Paige

Second, though much of the land of the Middle East is arid desert unsuitable for supporting farming, the land of

9

Canaan is located along the southwestern edge of the Fertile Crescent, offering access to rainfall and life-sustaining arable land. Dry summers and wet winters meant that planting occurred in the late fall and harvest in the early summer for staples such as barley, wheat, and flax. Other crops such as grapes, olives, figs, and dates were also main food sources in the area of Canaan, and more importantly, served as main exports for the region. In the ancient Middle East, grapes and olives were almost exclusively grown in the southern Levant, and therefore were highly valuable as wine and olive oil became luxury trade exports. This meant that not only did the land of Canaan function as a hub for trade, it also was the source of some of the most sought after goods, such as purple dye, wine, and olive oil.

With such abundant resources and access to land and sea trade routes, Canaan was a lucrative territory much sought after by surrounding empires. People groups moved into and through the region, conquering sites and despoiling local resources to support their forces. This means that the history of the inhabitants of Canaan is really the history of very different groups who found themselves for one reason or another residing in the land. The definition of a "Canaanite," or a resident of Canaan, was therefore never static; rather it shifted and changed as new groups moved into the region and assimilated with the local populations. For this reason, it is imperative that we study the history of the Canaanites in chronological order, focusing specifically on how these populations may have shifted or adapted over time. Throughout the subsequent chapters we will trace the history and culture of the Canaanites chronologically across several millennia from the Middle Bronze Age (1800 to 1550 BCE) to the Roman period (ca. 400 CE) in the region of the southern Levant. We will look closely at the textual and archaeological evidence that provides information about the languages, cultures, religions, and histories of the conglomeration of populations that are described in the ancient sources as "the Canaanites." We will also look in detail at how this history compares with and informs a reading of the biblical texts concerning this intriguing group.

2

THE EMERGENCE
OF THE CANAANITES

*(Early to Middle Bronze Age:
3200 to 1550 BCE)*

2.1 INTRODUCTION

ALTHOUGH THE BIBLICAL NARRATIVES interact with the
Canaanites for only a few hundred years, the pre-history
of the Canaanites in the region can be traced back several
millennia. Pre-history defines the period prior to written
history when Canaanites, or the inhabitants of Canaan,
can only be traced through archaeological evidence. The
Canaanites first feature prominently in historical sources
in the Late Bronze Age, roughly from 1550 BCE forward.
However, prior to this time, there were populations residing in the land of Canaan whose history undoubtedly had

an impact on the language, culture, religion, and ethnic make-up of the later populations.

Archaeological evidence suggests that populations continually inhabited the area of the southern Levant going back to at least the third millennium BCE. Jonathan Tubb has proposed that there is no significant disruption in settlement in the southern Levant, but rather that the material record from sites in the region shows continuity of settlement going back several millennia even before the Early Bronze Age II (3200 to 2500 BCE). Furthermore, numerous sites that were originally settled during the EB II period, especially those in the Cisjordan, remained inhabited throughout the Early Bronze III (2500 to 2200 BCE), Early Bronze IV (MB I/IBA) (2200 to 1800 BCE), and Middle Bronze periods (1800 to 1550 BCE). Though we have little knowledge regarding the ethnic make-up of the populations that inhabited these sites, this continuity of settlement does indicate that local populations remained in the region and did not migrate away even in the face of shifting political or ecological landscapes. Their perseverance was undoubtedly due, at least in part, to the advantageous position of Canaan, controlling major land and sea trade routes through the territory.

For these reasons, Tubb has proposed to define the term "Canaanite" as "the indigenous population of the Levant, the people who had always dwelt in that region since the time of the very earliest settled communities in remote prehistory."[1] Yet, archaeological evidence alone is not enough to support the hypothesis that Canaanites resided

1. Tubb, *Canaanites*, 13–14. Tubb proposes that continuity for the Canaanite population can be traced back to the eighth millennium in the Levant. Whether this is accurate, or whether a Canaanite population group migrated to the northern Levant at a later time is unknown.

in the land of Canaan continuously from the third millennium BCE. However, recent genetic research conducted in the southern Levant also lends credence to this conclusion. Excavations from the Middle Bronze Age settlement at the site of Sidon on the Lebanese coast have provided an important window into the history of the Canaanite populations. The team sampled DNA remains from the bones of five individuals who were interred at the site around 1600 BCE,[2] which were compared with the genetic sequences from individuals living in an Early Bronze Age cave above the site of ʿAin Ghazal in Jordan. Results from this phase of the research have shown that there is a close degree of genetic similarity between the two sources, despite being taken from skeletons separated by roughly fifteen hundred years. The team concluded that the same population had resided in the southern Levant beginning at least as early as the third millennium BCE and that "the different cultural groups who inhabited the Levant during the Bronze Age, such as the Ammonites, Moabites, Israelites, and Phoenicians, each achieved their own cultural identities but all shared a common genetic and ethnic root with Canaanites."[3] This genetic evidence provides support for the conclusion that the Canaanite population known from the Middle and Late Bronze Age was already in the area of the southern Levant by the Early Bronze Age.

2. Lawler, "Uncovering Sidon's Long Life."

3. Haber, Doumet-Serhal, Scheib, Xue, Danecek, et al., "Continuity and Admixture in the Last Five Millennia of Levantine History from Ancient Canaanite and Present-Day Lebanese Genome Sequences," 277.

2.2 EARLY BRONZE AGE II–III (3200 TO 2200 BCE)

This genetic evidence, when coupled with the archaeological evidence for the continuity of the populations, suggests that the pre-history of the inhabitants of the southern Levant extends back at least five thousand years into the third millennium BCE. Whether their presence in Canaan extends even further back into the fourth millennium or whether the original Canaanite populations migrated into the southern Levant at some point in the third millennium is unknown. Since we have no contemporaneous textual sources in the Early Bronze Age that refer to the terms "Canaan" or "Canaanite," any theories regarding the pre-historic emergence of Canaanites are ultimately unverifiable. But certainly for the writers and redactors of the Hebrew Bible, who were concerned with juxtaposing the protagonist Israelites with their foil the Canaanites, the land of Canaan and the Canaanites were treated as going back to even the earliest periods of cultural memory. Canaan and the Canaanites feature prominently in the patriarchal narratives. The patriarch Abraham is called to journey from Haran in the north to the land of Canaan in the south (Gen 11:19; 12:5–6), a land that was already inhabited by a distinct Canaanite population (Gen 12:5–6). Genesis 10:18–19 offers an Israelite account of the origin of this Canaanite population, calling them the descendants of Canaan, the grandson of Noah. Indeed, the biblical narrative goes out of its way to stress that the Canaanites were well established in the land of Canaan. This is significant for the biblical narrative, since the Canaanites were posed as the foil for Israel, and their land the divine inheritance for the nation of Abraham and his sons: "And I will give to you, and to your seed after you, the land of your wanderings, all the land of Canaan, as an everlasting possession" (Gen 17:8). Yet without clear extra-biblical textual evidence for the emergence of a Canaanite population back in the third millennium, the historical narrative of the Canaanites must begin in the Middle Bronze Age (ca. 1800 BCE) with the first textual evidence for the existence of this people group.[4]

The lack of written evidence makes it difficult to know much about the cultures or history of the Canaanites during this period. Fortunately, we do have access to archaeological data. Archaeological remains from the Early Bronze Age II–III period of the southern Levant tell of a flourishing society responsible for constructing massive structures such as the large temple enclosure and rounded altar found at Megiddo or the granary and city gate of Tel Bet Yerah near the Sea of Galilee in modern-day Israel.

The Early Bronze III period marks the pinnacle of the Canaanite civilizations in the pre-historical period. Sites are characterized by monumental architecture and expansive fortifications. However, this period of prosperous public works ended abruptly in the Early Bronze IV period, as sites were dramatically abandoned across the southern Levant.

2.3 EARLY BRONZE AGE IV (2200 TO 1800 BCE)

Over the past decade, climate research has allowed archaeologists to determine that a wide-scale climate shift impacted much of the Mediterranean and Near Eastern regions

---

4. The early biblical references to the emergence of the Canaanites in prehistoric periods are sparse and lacking detail. Furthermore, these references serve mainly the literary function of building the seemingly formidable history of the Canaanites. Even a conservative perspective of the biblical texts of the Pentateuch date these books to more than a millennium after the Early Bronze Age, making it difficult to rely upon scant references to the Canaanites as useful for constructing a firm history.

from about 2200 to 1800 BCE. Though the Mesopotamian heartland remained relatively stable during the period, northern Syria and the northern and southern Levant witnessed a three-hundred-year period of dramatically low precipitation. Climate estimates suggest that precipitation dropped abruptly by as much as 30 to 50 percent, causing cultivable land areas to narrow significantly, resulting in widespread site abandonment.[5]

During the Early Bronze IV period (MB I/IBA) from 2200 to 1800 BCE, the inhabitants of Canaan practiced increased economic specialization, turning to pastoral nomadism as a viable means of subsistence. Most sites were abandoned and the populations appear to turn to more nomadic lifestyles, tending large animal herds that moved around the region in search of water and grazing land. This nomadic landscape is reminiscent of the patriarchal narratives of the Hebrew Bible as Abraham and his nephew Lot are described as pitching their tents and tending their large flocks in the land of Canaan (Gen 13:12). The historicity of the Hebrew Bible is a complicated topic, and due to the nature of archaeological data, it is unlikely that written, contemporary extra-biblical sources will provide evidence for the existence of Abraham, Isaac, and Jacob. However, it is quite possible that the biblical patriarchal narratives preserve a culture memory of this period and the nomadic lifestyle that characterized the region during this time.

---

5. Weiss, "The Northern Levant during the Intermediate Bronze Age," 367. Weiss has shown that there existed a period of abrupt climate change characterized by low precipitation lasting from 4.2 to 3.9ka BP (2200 to 1900 BCE). Weiss notes that "this 300-year period provides, therefore, an alluring Holocene example of societal responses to abrupt climate change across the eastern Mediterranean and west Asian landscapes, and in particular across steep gradient ecotones of modern Syria and Lebanon."

But the land of Canaan was too valuable to remain uninhabited. The end of this period was marked by climate stabilization, as precipitation returned to its normal levels. The altered landscape of the period created a vacuum of centralized regional control, as urban sites no longer served as the center of rule in the region, as had been the case in the EB III period. This vacuum would be filled by both local populations and foreign migrations over the next several hundred years.

2.4 MIDDLE BRONZE AGE (1800 TO 1550 BCE)

With the return to climate stabilization, the Middle Bronze Age was characterized by a drastic return to urbanism. Populations returned to sites that had been abandoned for several centuries, and large public works were constructed. Like the Early Bronze Age III, in the Middle Bronze Age sites in the southern Levant were marked by massive building projects, including fortifications, large palace complexes, and temple structures. Sites such as Dan, Gezer, and Ashkelon feature large mudbrick city gates and fortification systems. (The gate at Dan is pictured below.) Other sites such as Shechem and Hazor include massive temple complexes. Though the picture below of the temple at Shechem does not look very imposing, this would have been a massive stone structure when it was built, with walls several meters thick and roof access allowing a view of the region. Such large building projects would have taken significant monetary and labor capital to construct, providing an indication that the Middle Bronze Age economy of Canaan was thriving during this period.

Figure 2.1: Middle Bronze Age mudbrick gate at the site of Dan
(ca. 1800 BCE)

Photo taken by author

Figure 2.2: Middle Bronze Age *migdal* temple at the site of Shechem
(ca. 1800 BCE)

Photo courtesy of Todd Bolen, BiblePlaces.com

Yet again, we are faced with the difficulty of equating archaeological finds with a specific population without supporting textual evidence. Some of these Middle Bronze Age sites share strong similarities with the previous sites of the Early Bronze period, providing some evidence that local Canaanite populations had constructed these urban centers. Other sites, especially those on the coast and along main trade routes, exhibit very different archaeological remains and patterns. In looking to explain this mixed landscape, Susan Cohen has suggested that such coastal fortified centers "imply an external orientation in the development of the region,"[6] meaning that these were likely the result of foreign influence, whether trade or migration. Another scholar, Aaron Burke, whose work focused on these Middle Bronze Age fortifications, has sought to define more precisely what this external orientation might be. He attributes the rise of urbanism in the Middle Bronze Age to peaceful Amorite migrations.[7]

In *The Amorite Dynasty of Ugarit*, I argue that the same constellation of material remains that appear at Amorite sites in the northern Levant such as Mari, Alalaḫ, and Ugarit is replicated at sites in the southern Levant such as Megiddo, Hazor, and Shechem. This Amorite material assemblage includes five key elements: large fortification systems, a unique palace organizational system (including a throne room and audience suite), monumental temples with massive towers, Amorite-style haematite seals, and finally the literary and archaeological evidence for the ritual use of donkeys.

6. Cohen, *Canaanites, Chronologies, and Connections*, 128.

7. Burke, "*Walled Up to Heaven*," 96–100, 160. Burke describes the Middle Bronze II B–C period in the Levant as a period of "Pax Amoritica" where independent Amorite kin-based groups ruled the Levant, establishing a series of trade networks between sites.

All of these features were unique to the northern Levantine Amorite sites, but gradually spread south into the land of Canaan during the course of the Middle Bronze Age. The appearance of this constellation of material remains so far from the Amorite homeland suggests that Amorites migrated into the southern Levant, intermingling with the local population. These migrating Amorite populations brought with them distinct elements of their material assemblage that reflected aspects of social complexity, religious expression, and administrative practices. Below is a map of the appearance of this material assemblage from the middle Euphrates region into the southern Levant.

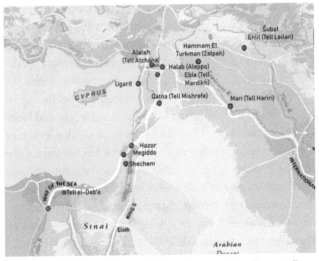

Figure 2.3: Map of sites exhibiting elements of the "Amorite" material assemblage
Map created by Dillon Paige

From the map, it is clear that this material assemblage only appears at a limited number of sites. Since only a few sites in the southern Levant exhibit features characteristic of Amorite populations, it is likely that Amorite migratory kin-based groups did not take over the entire region. Rather, the sites that have yielded evidence of Amorite migration are located at key positions affording access to local trade routes, including Hazor, Shechem, and Megiddo. The Amorite kin-based groups that settled these sites then interacted with the indigenous Canaanite populations, perhaps stimulating smaller sites to expand and develop in response to increased trade and cultural exchange.

The level of interaction between these larger Amorite sites and the indigenous population is ultimately unclear. These Amorite groups may have peaceably infiltrated the region, bringing with them increased economic specialization and trade, or they may have arrived in force, imposing a political network of control over the surrounding sites. Though it is unclear what this interaction may have been, it is clear that this expansion had a significant impact on the land of Canaan. Large urban centers cropped up across the southern Levant, most of which feature large public works, which would have required substantial monetary and labor capital to construct. Over fifty sites have yielded evidence for fortification systems in the southern Levant during the Middle Bronze Age.[8] Whether these fortifications systems were constructed as a defensive mechanism from external invaders, or they were a means chosen by local Canaanite rulers to showcase their weight and power, is unclear. However, what is clear is that large fortification systems and urban centers became a hallmark of Canaanite culture in the southern Levant in the Middle Bronze Age.

8. Burke, "The Architecture of Defense: Fortified Settlements of the Levant during the Middle Bronze Age," Appendix B. A total of fifty sites have yielded sure evidence of fortification in the MB IIB-C period, but have not yielded any further evidence of the Amorite material assemblage discussed here.

While the archaeological evidence supports the migration of Amorite populations and the rise of Canaanite urban centers, we also have some limited textual evidence for the word "Canaanite" being used to describe at least some of the residents in the region. The first and only reference to the Canaanites in the Middle Bronze Age is found in the Mari Archives. Mari was a major urban center in the central Euphrates area ruled by Amorite kings, the excavations of which have uncovered more than twenty-five thousand tablets and fragments providing invaluable insight into the period. The reference to the Canaanites is found in a letter written from a certain Mut-Bisir to king Šamši–Addu of Mari,[9] dated to the year 1778 BCE, two years before Yasmaʿ-Addu would be ousted by Zimri-Lîm.[10] Mut-Bisir provides an account of the status of several towns and communities in the southern Levant, including the *Kinaḫnūm* who were then residing in the town of Raḫiṣum.[11] Raḫiṣum has been equated with the town Ruḫizzi known from the Amarna letters,[12] which was likely located near the city of Qadesh (Tell Nebi Mend), a city in the land of Canaan. Unfortunately, no further references to the "Canaanites" or the "land of Canaan" are found in the Middle Bronze Age, so

9. Dossin, "Une mention de Cananéens dans une lettre de Mari." The letter is text A.3552, which was discovered at the site of Mari.

10. Charpin and Ziegler, *Mari et le Proche-Orient à l'époque amorrite*, 150.

11. Durand, *Documents épistolaires du palais de Mari, tome II*, 29–31. A.3552:9'–10'. Durand has translated these two lines as following: "Des gitans et des gens du pays de Canaʾan se sont installés dans Raḫiṣum même," referring to the *Ḫabbatūm* as "gypsies" or as wandering travelers, and to the *Kinaḫnūm* as the men of Canaan. The town Raḫiṣum only occurs in this one text from the Mari archives, so identification for the location of this town must be found in later sources.

12. Durand, "Villes fantômes de Syrie et autres lieux."

few conclusions can be drawn as to the geographic extent or ethnic makeup of this group. However, what is clear is that already by 1776 BCE, foreign populations were aware of Canaanites residing in the area of the southern Levant.

It is also in this time period that we get the first glimpse of what Canaanites may have looked like. In a tomb found at Beni Hasan, a site in Egypt used for burial in the Middle Kingdom. In the tomb of nobleman Khnumhotep II, wall paintings are found depicting many scenes including work crews, Nile river scenes, and Khnumhotep himself receiving offerings. One of these scenes depicts "Asiatics," the term used by the Egyptians to refer to the populations of the land of Canaan, bringing black eye-paint to Khnumhotep. Below is an artist's reproduction of this scene of Canaanites as well as a photograph of the original tomb painting so as to clearly see the Canaanite procession.

Figure 2.4: Beni Hasan Tomb 3, Canaanite scene, artist's reconstruction

(C. R. Lepsius, *Denkmäler aus Aegypten und Aethiopien.* Ergänzungband
[Giza plates only]
[Berlin: Nicolaische Buchhandlung. Leipzig: Hinrichs'sche, 1913].)

Figure 2.5: Photo of Canaanite scene on wall of Beni Hasan Tomb 3
Photo courtesy of A.D. Riddle, BiblePlaces.com

The scene provides a small window into the culture of the Middle Bronze Age Asiatics or Canaanites in terms of dress, weaponry, appearance, and even gender. First, the Canaanites are depicted as traders bringing ingredients for black eye-paint to Egypt, indicating there was some type of lucrative relationship between Khnumhotep and the

Canaanite traders. Galena, or lead ore, was the chief substance used to create black eye-paint commonly worn in Egypt, and would likely have been mined along the Red Sea.[13] Whether the traders actually mined the substance, or simply served as nomadic middle-men, is unknown. The use of kohl or eye makeup was both fashionable and functional. While the paint served to enhance beauty and may have even carried religious significance, the paint was also slathered liberally around the eyes to reduce glare from the sun. From this wall painting, and from other depictions of Canaanites, it appears that kohl was also worn by Canaanites, and was an integral part of appearance in the ancient world.

While both Egyptians and Canaanites may have applied kohl, other elements of their appearance vary quite drastically. Unlike the Egyptians, who are portrayed as clean shaven, the Canaanites are shown consistently with beards. Both men and women are dressed in multi-colored, patterned garments, each of which appears to have a unique pattern, perhaps indicating the Canaanites had a rich weaving industry. These garments were likely made of wool, which was quite distinct from the white linen garments favored in ancient Egypt.

Several other implements are also depicted, including musical instruments and weapons such as spears, axes, and a bow and arrows. One of the men is also holding a small hand-held stringed instrument or harp, which may either be a gift that he was bringing or perhaps indicates that the Canaanite traders enjoyed music while on the road. Notably, only the men in the image, as well as one of the male children, are seen holding the weapons, and appear to be flanking the women in the group. Military history experts

13. Cohen, "Interpretative Uses and Abuses of the Beni Hasan Tomb Painting," 34.

of the Levant find the bow and arrow depicted in the Beni Hassan tomb painting to be especially significant since it provides the first evidence for the use of the composite bow in the area of the Levant. The composite bow had a more powerful draw, which allowed archers to shoot arrows with heavier points at a greater range and with increased accuracy.[14]

There are also four women depicted in the image, who appear to be grouped together. As noted, the women hold no weapons or instruments, and appear to be at the center of the caravan. The women have longer hair, secured by bands, and wear full-length garments with complex colored patterns. Their feet are painted red, and it appears that they are wearing boots, which is rare, as very few examples of boots are found in artistic renderings from this period. Both Egyptian and Canaanite men are depicted as either barefoot or wearing light sandals, so these are the only four individuals wearing boots. Ahead of the women, are also several children, either walking or riding the donkey, indicating that whole families of traders made the journey to bring goods to Egypt.

Later Egyptian depictions of Canaanites from the New Kingdom, roughly corresponding to the Late Bronze Age, similarly represent Canaanites with beards and striped garments. Perhaps one of the more famous images of a Canaanite is found in the Book of the Gates from the New Kingdom, corresponding to the Late Bronze Age in the Levant. The Book of the Gates includes a depiction of souls in procession passing into the next world. In this procession, the four races of the world, as conceived from the Egyptian perspective, are portrayed. Here, alongside a Libyan, Nubian, and an Egyptian, a Canaanite is shown with a beard and a colored and patterned kilt.

14. Burke, *"Walled Up to Heaven,"* 33–35.

Figure 2.6: Four races of the world: Libyan, Nubian, Asiatic (Canaanite), and Egyptian

Illustration by unknown author, copy by Heinrich Menu von Minutoli, and reproduced in E. Hornung, *The Ancient Egyptian Books of the Afterlife* (translated by D. Lorton; Ithaca, NY: Cornell University Press, 1999).

From the perspective of the ancient Egyptians, each of the four main population groups had specific physical and cultural characteristics. Skin color, hair length and color, clothing and headdress styles, facial hair, jewelry, tattoos, and physical features are all distinct for each of the peoples included here. The similarity between this painting and that from Beni Hasan, separated temporally by roughly five hundred years, highlights the strong continuity between the Canaanites of the Middle Bronze Age and those of the Late Bronze Age. This continuity emphasizes the imperative of viewing the Canaanites in their historical context. Traditions of dress and even personal grooming continued largely unchanged among the Canaanite populations of the southern Levant.

The Middle Bronze Age represents the golden age of the Canaanite populations of the southern Levant, as they settled large urban centers and benefited from trade with Middle Kingdom Egypt (2050 to 1550 BCE) to the south. Unlike the transition from the EB III to the EB IV periods, where the southern Levant changed dramatically with populations abandoning urban sites in favor of nomadic pastoralism, there is an almost seamless transition between the Middle Bronze to the Late Bronze Age. Canaanite populations continued to reside in the land of Canaan, and much of their culture, such as their dress and appearance, as seen above, would continue throughout the Late Bronze Age. The primary change is that these Canaanite populations would lose the autonomy they enjoyed in the Middle Bronze Age, as larger empires, including those of Hatti, Egypt, and Ugarit, would take control of the region.

3

CANAANITES UNDER EGYPTIAN RULE

(Late Bronze Age: 1550 to 1200 BCE)

FOR A QUARTER OF a millennium during the Middle Bronze Age (1800 to 1550 BCE) the Canaanites enjoyed relative autonomy in the region of the southern Levant with few foreign interventions. Though there was trade between Canaan and Egypt during this period, the Egyptian dynasties of the Second Intermediate period were relatively small and did not make political conquests beyond the Sinai Peninsula. However, this level of autonomy would quickly be stripped away in the Late Bronze Age. Canaanite tribal groups continued to reside in the land of Canaan, and for the most part continued to inhabit their walled urban centers, which had been established in the Middle Bronze Age. Indeed, the transition from the Middle to the Late Bronze Age in the southern Levant is not marked by a drastic change in the archaeological record; rather there is a significant degree of continuity through the period. The shift between these two periods was in reality a *political* one, as Canaan was conquered and controlled by the New Kingdom of Egypt.

3.1 POLITICAL LANDSCAPE

During the New Kingdom period, Egypt increased its territory to the largest extent in Egyptian history, encompassing all of the land of Canaan to the north and stretching south into Nubia. The New Kingdom witnessed the rise of some of the most famous and enigmatic pharaohs in the history of Egypt, such as Hatshepsut, the second female pharaoh of Egypt, Thutmose III who would campaign into Canaan seventeen times, Akhenaten who was responsible for the creation of the Aten cult, and finally the boy king, Tutankhamun, who would die at just nineteen.

Concurrent with the rise of the New Kingdom in Egypt, other major empires arose across the ancient Middle East. The kingdom of Hatti, ruled by the Hittites, emerged as a formidable military power in the territory of Asia Minor (modern-day Turkey). The Hittites first rose to prominence in 1595 BCE when Mursili I led his forces from the Hittite homeland all the way to Babylon, sacking the great Amorite kingdoms of the Middle Bronze Age. Then, following a several-hundred-year period of weakness, the Hittite New Kingdom would again become a major political force in the region from 1400 to 1200 BCE, with powerful military rulers such as Suppiluliuma I, who challenged Egyptian dominance. To the south of Hatti was the kingdom of Ugarit, whose political affiliation often wavered between Egypt and Hatti, but their access to major ports provided wealth enough to make them a relatively major player on the international stage. In the Mesopotamia heartland, other empires such as the Mittani, Assyria, the Kassites, and Elam also arose, and a period of international relations characterized by international trade and diplomacy was established. The kings of these empires were known as "great kings," who corresponded and traded with one another in a high point of international cooperation in the ancient Middle East. Though borders were constantly shifting, these large empires controlled much of the known world for over a quarter of a millennium throughout the Late Bronze Age (1550 to 1200 BCE), as shown in Figure 3.1.

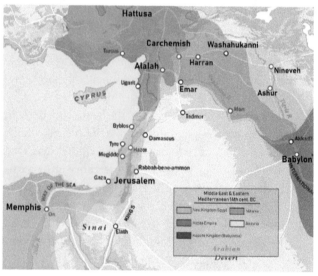

Figure 3.1: Map of the Great Kings of the Late Bronze Age
Map created by Dillon Paige

For roughly 250 years, throughout the eighteenth and nineteenth dynasties of the New Kingdom, Egypt would maintain strong political control over the land of Canaan. The first textual reference to the Canaanites in Egyptian texts comes from the reign of Amenhotep II (1427 to 1400), who is recorded as bringing 640 Canaanite ("*ki-na-ʿ-nu*") captives to Memphis in Egypt following his very first Asiatic campaign in the initial year of his reign.[1] Throughout the eighteenth and nineteenth dynasties Egypt continued to make military conquests into the land of Canaan, frequently bringing captives into the Egyptian heartland. Such military control ensured that Canaan would not rebel, allowing Egypt to retain the much-needed buffer zone between themselves and Hatti to the north. Figures 3.2 and 3.3 show Canaanites being led captive and struck by Egyptian pharaohs of the New Kingdom.

Figure 3.2: Canaanite captives on Ramesses II statue, Luxor Temple
Photo taken by the author

1. Hoffmeier, "The Memphis and Karnak Stelae of Amenhotep II (2.3)."

33

**Figure 3.3: Seti I triumphal scene holding Canaanite captives
by the hair**
Photo taken by the author

Following the conquest of Canaan by the hands of Pharaoh Thutmose III, Egypt established military outposts at sites such as Gaza, Jaffa, and Tell Beth She'an, the last of which occupied a strategic position which controlled both the Jordan River Valley and the Jezreel Valley. Remains of an Egyptian governor's mansion were uncovered as well as evidence of a substantial military presence at the site,[2] which guaranteed that the local Canaanite populations remained in check. Maintaining political oversight of Canaan ensured that Egypt had control of key trade routes but also provided a buffer zone protecting Egypt from the kingdoms to the north, such as Hatti.

2. Mazar, "The Egyptian Garrison Town of Beth-Shean."

Figure 3.4: Governor's mansion on the acropolis of Tell Beit She'an
Photo courtesy of Todd Bolen, BiblePlaces.com

In addition to political control, Egypt also valued Canaan for its resources, including grain, olive oil, wine, and other raw materials. Perhaps the most valued resource available in Canaan was copper as the site of Timna in the Negev Desert boasts some of the richest copper mines in the world. Indeed, greenish-hew rocks with copper ore are still visible on the surface of the land in Timna today. During the Late Bronze Age, Egypt not only controlled the copper mines at Timna, but also employed Egyptian workers to extract the goods. These Egyptian workers brought with them their mining skill, but also brought their culture and religion. A temple to the goddess Hathor constructed at Timna for the local Egyptian workers attests the Egyptian presence in the area.

Figure 3.5: Temple of the goddess Hathor at the site of Timna
Photo courtesy of Todd Bolen, BiblePlaces.com

In addition to raw materials, Egypt also extracted tribute from the local Canaanite rulers. The political outposts such as the one at Beit She'an also served as centers for the collection of tribute and taxes. The regular payment of such tribute ensured that the Canaanite tribal groups would receive military protection from Egypt in the event of war with other local tribal groups or when facing threats from Hatti to the north.

3.2 HISTORICAL SOURCES

Unlike the Middle Bronze Age, for which we only have one scant textual source alluding to the Canaanites, the Late Bronze Age witnesses a burgeoning of historical documents that provide valuable insight into the territory, culture, and language of the Canaanites. The earliest textual references to Canaan appear at the start of the Late Bronze Age and emphasize that by 1500 BCE Canaan was perceived as a distinct geopolitical entity in the political landscape. Two texts referring to the land of Canaan have been found at the site of Alalaḫ located in modern-day Turkey.[3] Legal text AT 48:4–5 records a large debt owed by "Baʻlaya, a man of the city of Canaan" whose wife and children would stand as pledge until the debt was repaid. Naʼaman has argued that it is the legal nature of this text that lends credence to the perspective that Canaan was understood as a distinct entity at the time of the Alalaḫ IV corpus (ca. 1500 to 1450 BCE).[4] Another early reference to the land of Canaan is found in the Idrimi statue (ca. 1500 BCE). Idrimi records his flight from Emar into the coastal Levantine region: "I came to the land of Canaan. The city of Ammiya is located in the land of Canaan" (*a-na ma-at Ki-in-a-ni₇*KI / *al-li-ik i-na ma-at Ki-in-a-ni₇*KI / URU *Am-mi-ia*KI).[5] The city of Ammiya is likely to be equated with the modern-day city of Amyûn near Byblos in Lebanon,[6] suggesting that the territory of Canaan encompassed the Phoenician coastal cities of modern Lebanon.

While we see references to both Canaan and the Canaanites in textual sources from both Egypt and Alalaḫ, undoubtedly the most valuable historical source for the period comes from the site of Tell el-ʻAmarna in Egypt. In 1887, a cache of over 350 letters as well as thirty-two other documents was discovered at the site. The letters cover roughly a one-hundred-year period, spanning several pharaohs of the New Kingdom, and document political

3. Wiseman, *The Alalakh Tablets*, 46, 71. Text AT 48:4–5 records the existence of "Baʻlaya, a man of the city of Canaan" and text AT 181:9 makes reference to "Šarniya, a son of the land of Canaan."

4. Naʼaman, "Four Notes on the Size of Late Bronze Age Canaan," 32.

5. Smith, *The Statue of Idri-mi*, plate 9–10. Stele of Idrimi, lines 18–20.

6. Rainey, "Who Is a Canaanite? A Review of the Textual Evidence," 4.

relationships between Egypt, Canaan, and the rest of the great kings of the period. Of the 350 letters, forty-five are written from other great kings in the region (such as Babylon, Hatti, etc.), seven are written by an Egyptian pharaoh, and the rest are written by local Canaanite rulers. It is from these letters written by Canaanite rulers that we gain the greatest insight into the culture and language of Canaan.

**Figure 3.6: Amarna Letter written in Akkadian script
on a clay tablet**
Photo courtesy of A.D. Riddle, BiblePlaces.com

The terms "Canaan" and "Canaanite" are mentioned twelve times in the Amarna letters,[7] all of which appear to

7. EA 8:13–21,25; EA 9:19–21; EA 14: II, 26; EA 30:1–2; EA 36:15 (reading *ki-na-'i* is uncertain, but likely references the land of

refer to a distinct geopolitical entity with which the great kings of the period would interact. Burna-Burriaš, the Kassite ruler of Babylon in the mid-fourteenth century, corresponded with the Canaanite rulers of the southern Levant. He recalls a time when the Canaanite rulers called upon Babylon for support: "In (the reign of) Kurigalzu,[8] my predecessor, all the Canaanites wrote to him saying: 'Come to the border of the country, so we can revolt and become your allies.'"[9] The Mitannian king also wrote to the "kings of the land of Canaan, the servants of my brother (Egypt)" to grant safe passage to his ambassador, who had been dispatched on a mission to Egypt.[10] These references indicate that though the individual Canaanite kings ruled over autonomous, and relatively insignificant, territories in Canaan, which frequently were at war with one another, from an external perspective, they were perceived as a geopolitical unit. Furthermore, we learn that life under Egyptian rule was taxing enough to warrant seeking allies to throw off the Egyptian yoke.

Yet while Egyptian taxes may have been burdensome, Egypt also provided valuable political and military support when called upon. One Akkadian letter found at Ugarit makes reference to a court case between the "sons of Ugarit" and the "sons of Canaan."[11] In the letter, the court of Ugarit

---

Canaan); EA 109:44–46; EA 110:48–49 (reading *ki-na-[áʾ-ni]* is again very uncertain); EA 137:75–76; EA 148:39–47; EA 151: 49–67; EA 162:40–41; EA 367:7–8.

8. Clayden, "Dūr-Kurigalzu: New Perspectives," 437. The Kassite ruler of Babylon, Kurigalzu, reigned through the first part of the fourteenth century, ending ca. 1375 BCE.

9. Rainey, "Who Is a Canaanite?" 7. EA 9:19–21.

10. Moran, *The Amarna Letters*, 100. EA 30:1–2.

11. Lackenbacher, Ugaritica V no. 36. 51. RS 20.182+20.181. Lines 5 and 6 include the ethnic terminology "sons of Ugarit" and "sons of Canaan."

addresses the Egyptian pharaoh, confirming that reparation has been paid to the "sons of Canaan" whose caravan had been seized in the kingdom of Ugarit. Though details of the case are sparse, it is clear that Egypt had stepped in on behalf of the Canaanite traders to arbitrate the case. As Na'aman has noted, the very fact that the Ugaritic court was corresponding with the Egyptian pharaoh suggests that Egypt had mediated the case since "Canaan was the territory of the Pharaoh, and it was his responsibility to protect his vassals in the other Great Kings' lands and to defend their rights in foreign countries."[12] Though details surrounding the seizure of the Canaanite caravan are scarce, relations between Ugarit and Canaan to the south were sufficiently hostile that not only was the Canaanite caravan seized upon entering Ugaritian territory, but Egypt was forced to step in to ensure justice and payment of reparation.

While other major empires such as Ugarit, Babylon, Mitanni, and Egypt all referred to the populations of the land of Canaan as "Canaanites," this term was never adopted by the Canaanite rulers themselves. Rather, they represented themselves as independent monarchs who ruled over semi-autonomous kingdoms and whose affiliation was to their local tribe or location, as opposed to some larger concept of Canaan. Indeed, relations between these local Canaanite rulers were often fraught with tension. Numerous Amarna letters record these violent interactions.

12. Na'aman, "Four Notes on the Size of Late Bronze Age Canaan," 35.

El Amarna Letter 364

To the king, my lord: Message of Ayyab, your servant, . . . I have guarded very carefully [the citie]s of the king, my Lord. Moreover, note that it is the ruler of Ḫaṣura who has taken three cities from me. From the time I heard and verified this, there has been waging of war against him. Truly, may the king, my lord, take cognizance, and may the king, my lord, give thought to his servant.

El Amarna Letter 125

To the king, my lord: Message of Rib-Hadda, [your] ser[vant], . . . Previously there was a garrison of the king with me, and the king was accustomed to give grain for their food. But now, Aziru has repeatedly raided me. I have neither oxen nor sheep and goats. Aziru has taken everything. And there is no grain for my food, and the peasantry has gone off to towns where there is grain for their food.

These two letters were both written from local Canaanite rulers to the Egyptian pharaoh requesting either military reinforcements or food, since other Canaanite tribal leaders had attacked and raided them. From these letters we learn that while Egypt gained resources, tribute, and a military buffer zone in Canaan, the pharaohs were fatigued by frequent requests for help in arbitrating matters. In fact, over fifty sites are mentioned in the Amarna Letters as shown in the map below, indicating that while Egypt may have controlled the region, the political landscape was one of warring local Canaanite tribes.

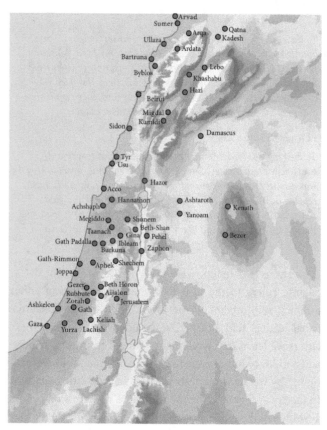

Figure 3.7: Map of all sites in the land of Canaan mentioned
in the Amarna Letters
Map created by Dillon Paige

This period of international relations and Egyptian control of Canaan provides the backdrop for the emergence of Israel. According to the biblical narratives, following forty years of desert wanderings, Israel moved through the Transjordan with the goal of crossing into the promised land of Canaan.[13] After burning the sites of Hazor, Ai, and Jericho, the Israelites moved in to settle the land of Canaan. The narrative of the book of Joshua speaks of almost complete conquest of the land,[14] yet the book of Judges opens to a far more complicated political landscape: "After the death of Joshua the sons of Israel asked of Yʜwʜ saying, 'who shall go up for us at first against the Canaanite to do battle with them?'" (Judg 1:1). The book of Judges depicts the land of Canaan not as a single territory under the rule of Israel, but rather as a mixed landscape of smaller tribes: "The children of Israel dwelt among the Canaanites, Hittites, Amorites, Perizzites, Hivites, and Jebusites" (Judg 1:4). Certainly in the period of the Late Bronze Age, Canaanite tribal groups dominated the region of the southern Levant. Yet, as discussed previously, these tribes never

13 The historicity of the emergence of Israel is a hotly debated topic amongst scholarship. Conservative scholars link the destruction of sites such as Jericho and Hazor at the end of the Middle Bronze Age with the Israelite conquest as depicted in the biblical narratives (Bimson, *Redating the Exodus and Conquest*). Other scholars believe that Israel emerged as a distinct entity in opposition to the Philistine populations on the coastline during the transition from the Late Bronze Age to the Iron Age (Faust, *Israel's Ethnogenesis*, 168–69). Still others believe that Israel emerged later in the Iron Age such as around the time of King David in the tenth century BCE (Garfinkel, *The Prehistory of Israel*), or even later with the rise of the Omride dynasty in Israel in the ninth century BCE. This brief review of scholarship showcases that there is little consensus around the timing for the emergence of Israel. From a literary perspective, the biblical narratives themselves present Israel as a fully-formed people group moving into the promised land of Canaan perhaps at the start of the Late Bronze Age, facing the formidable enemy of the Canaanite tribes dwelling in the region.

14. There are a few hints in the book of Joshua that the conquest was not as complete as it appeared and that the people of Israel did not completely drive out the Canaanites from the land. E.g., "They did not disposes the Canaanites, the ones dwelling in Gezer. So the Canaanites dwelt in the midst of Ephraim until this day" (Josh 16:10).

identified themselves as Canaanites, preferring to associate themselves with their local tribal group. Over the course of the next several hundred years, these tribal groups would grow increasingly more distinct as smaller kingdoms would break off and develop their own unique languages, cultures, and religions. These groups were the Israelites, Moabites, Ammonites, etc., who feature so prominently in the biblical narrative.

3.3 CANAANITE LANGUAGES

While the Amarna letters provide insight into the historical and political landscape of the land of Canaan, they also provide evidence for the language that was spoken in the region. The lingua franca of the day was an East Semitic dialect known as Babylonian written in the cuneiform script. This common language allowed rulers from across the ancient Middle East to correspond. However, while the letters from the Canaanite rulers are written in the cuneiform script, the underlying language is a bit of a mixed, pidgin dialect. The lexemes are primarily Babylonian, but the grammar and verbal systems are written in a West Semitic language.[15] This West Semitic language is known as Amarna Canaanite and provides insight into the language spoken by the Canaanites in the Late Bronze Age.

Though Amarna Canaanite is the first significant corpus of Canaanite material that provides evidence for the Canaanite languages, there is some evidence, albeit limited, that Canaanite may have emerged as a distinct language family as early as the end of the Middle Bronze Age. One defining feature of the Canaanite languages is a sound change from ā > ō known as the Canaanite Shift. From the transcription of West Semitic words and toponyms in

15. Moran, *The Amarna Letters*, xxi–xxii.

Egyptian sources, Hoch has shown that there is consistent appearance of the Canaanite Shift beginning in the reign of Thutmose III (1480 to 1425 BCE). This evidence suggests that the Canaanite Shift was fully in play by 1500 BCE, and that, therefore, Canaanite had to have emerged as a distinct language family at the end of the Middle Bronze Age.

Already by the Late Bronze Age, the Canaanite language was distinct from the Ugaritic and Amorite languages to the north, and it is likely that, though dialect variations undoubtedly existed, the Canaanite rulers were able to communicate with one another using this language. Over the course of the next several hundred years, regional dialectal variations would continue to increase, as new languages such as Hebrew, Phoenician, Moabite, Ammonite, and others would develop as distinct languages in the Canaanite language family.

3.4 CANAANITE RELIGION

Outside of textual sources, we have evidence for other aspects of Canaanite culture from the archaeological record. It is worth noting that while numerous scholars have tried to draw close parallels between Canaanite religion and the site of Ugarit, the historical discussion up to this point highlights the need to keep these distinct. Canaan was a distinct geopolitical region with its own language and its own culture from the Middle to the Late Bronze Age. Similarly, Ugarit finds its roots in the Amorite culture of the Middle Bronze Age, developing independently from its Canaanite neighbors in the southern Levant. While there are certainly parallels to be drawn between the cultures of Canaan and Ugarit, it is essential to view these as distinct regions with rich and varied histories of cultural development.

Several Canaanite urban centers, such as Gezer and Hazor, that were settled in the Middle Bronze Age remained inhabited in the Late Bronze Age and have yielded significant archaeological material showcasing Canaanite religion. One of the most striking cultic finds from the site of Gezer are the massive standing stones occupying the center of the site pictured below. There are ten stones in total, each weighing upwards of several tons, with the tallest stone measuring roughly three meters or almost ten feet. The stones were erected in a line on the north/south access, and were accompanied by large stone basin measuring six feet by five feet. The exact function of the stones is unknown, though based upon finds around the area, it is likely that these served as a cultic worship area for the population in and around Gezer. Similar standing stones are also known from other sites such as Shechem, suggesting that such outdoor corporate worship sites were common in the period.

Figure 3.8: Standing stones and libation trough at the site of Gezer
Photo taken by author

In addition to outdoor cultic areas, other sites have yielded evidence for interior cultic worship centers. Area C at Hazor is perhaps the best example of a small interior temple. Around the walls of the Hazor temple are benches, which would have allowed for worshippers to gather. At the focal point of the temple are eleven stelae made of basalt, including standing stones, a statue of a seated male figure, a lion statue, and a basin used for libation offerings as shown below.[16] Based upon iconography on the chest of the seated figure, it is likely that this was a statue to the storm god Baʻal known from the Hebrew Bible and Ugarit. Since the shrine was inside and located near the main palace complex it is possible that this served the residential area and may provide clues about local private cultic practice.

Figure 3.9: Standing stones from Area C temple at the site of Hazor
Photo courtesy of Todd Bolen, BiblePlaces.com

16. Greener, "Archaeology and Religion in Late Bronze Age Canaan," 9–10.

Figurines of deities, like the seated Ba'al statue from Hazor, have been discovered at sites throughout Late Bronze Age Canaan providing clues regarding the Canaanite pantheon. Figures are usually standing or seated and are often found in cultic contexts indicating they were part of local worship practices. At Megiddo a bronze statue with gold leaf of a seated deity—likely El, the head of the pantheon—was found. In addition to figures of male deities, figurines of female deities have also been uncovered. Small figures of the naked female form in both clay and metal have been uncovered at several Late Bronze Age Canaanite sites such as the one from Tell Batash pictured below.[17] Though it is difficult to know for sure which deity or deities these figurines represented it is likely that, due to the prominence of the female organs in the depictions, as well as other symbols of fertility, such as leaves and trees, that these represented the fertility goddess Asherah.

Figure 3.10: Statue of El from Megiddo
Photo courtesy of the Oriental Institute Museum

Figure 3.11: Statue of El (or Ba'al) from Hazor
Photo courtesy of Todd Bolen, BiblePlaces.com

Figure 3.12: Statue of Asherah from Tell Batash
Photo courtesy of A.D. Riddle, BiblePlaces.com

17. Greener, "Archaeology and Religion in Late Bronze Age Canaan," 11–14.

The presence of figurines depicting the head deities of the pantheon such as Baʿal, the storm god, El, the head of the pantheon, and Asherah, the mother goddess of fertility, showcase the active religious cult of the Canaanites. This is also reminiscent of the biblical narrative, where the people of Israel were rebuked for going after the gods of the Canaanites: "they abandoned YHWH and served Baʿal and the Ashtarot" (Judg 2:13). The worship of this Canaanite pantheon would continue to flourish, even after the fall of the Late Bronze Age, which will be described in the following chapter.

3.5 CANAANITE DAILY LIFE

Certainly politics, warfare, and religion were significant aspects of daily life in Canaan. However, while kings warred with one another, and Egyptian overlords ensured regular tribute, daily life of the average Canaanite family continued. The lifestyle in Bronze Age Canaan would have been primarily agrarian and would have therefore been heavily dictated by the weather, seasonal change, and harvests. The Gezer Calendar, a brief text written in a Canaanite language from the tenth century BCE pictured in Figure 3.13 below, provides evidence as to the farming schedule in an agrarian community in Canaan.

Figure 3.13: Gezer Calendar
Photo courtesy of Todd Bolen, BiblePlaces.com

Text Translation	Corresponding Month
Two months—ingathering.	September–October
Two months—sowing.	November–December
Two months—late sowing.	January–February
Month—flax cutting.	March
Month—barley harvest.	April
Month—harvest & completion.	May
Two months—vine harvest.	June–July
Month—summer.	August

The life of the family and the community would have been consumed with these regular sowing and harvesting cycles. Also, since dry farming was practiced in the southern Levant in the Bronze Age, rather than irrigation, communities would have been eagerly awaiting the three rainy cycles in the year, which came in early fall, midwinter, and early spring, without which they would have no harvest. The text above also provides a window into the crops of the region of the southern Levant. Wheat, flax, and barley made up the staple crops, as well as dates, grapes, olives, and almonds, which supplemented their diet and provided natural sweetener.

In addition to farming, there were other important household activities that were central to daily life in Bronze Age Canaan. Textile production, either for use or for export, was one activity that was practiced inside the home. Woven fabrics are rarely preserved in archaeological context, but other elements of the weaving industry are preserved inside homes such loom weights, spindle whorls, awls, or needles. Also present are remains of beads or buttons, which were used for adornment on garments.[18]

Food and drink production were conducted inside the home and would have consumed a large part of each day's schedule. Following the harvest and threshing, grain needed to be ground for use. Grinding stones are found in home contexts, where they were used for grinding the grain to create baked goods or beer. A stela from Tell el-Amarna during the New Kingdom in Egypt shown in Figure 3.14 below features a man, who is depicted in the standard Canaanite style with beard, curly hair, and colored and patterned garment, along with a woman and a servant depicted in the standard Egyptian style, though both the man and the woman are given Canaanite names. In the scene the man is depicted drinking beer from a very long straw. Though the drinking straw originated in Mesopotamia, based upon artistic depictions and archaeological

18. Ebeling, "Women's Daily Life in Bronze Age Canaan," 468–70.

remains, the use of the straw spread into the Levant and subsequently into Egypt during the Late Bronze Age, and greatly facilitated the consumption of beer.[19]

**Figure 3.14: Stela from Tell el-Amarna featuring
a Canaanite drinking beer
Berlin 14122[20]**

While farming, textile manufacturing, and food and drink production were key aspects of daily life in Bronze Age Canaan, perhaps the most prominent aspect of life may have been death. In a study of more than four hundred burials of Late Bronze Age Canaan, Kennedy has found that the

19. Sparks, "Canaan in Egypt: Archaeological Evidence for a Social Phenomenon," 37.

20. Brovarsky, Doll, Freed, *Egypt's Golden Age*, 109 figure 34.

average life expectancy would have been between twenty-five and thirty-seven years, and that roughly only 3 percent of the population would have made it past the age of sixty. Life spans were far shorter, due to harsh living conditions, polluted water, and poor medical care. Furthermore, infant mortality was a regular part of life, with roughly 20 percent of all children dying in infancy.[21]

With such high mortality rates, death and burial became an important part of life. Burials in Canaan in the Late Bronze Age are typically of two types: "pit burials for individual interment and cave burials for multiple interment," with pit burials being the more common type.[22] Both practices are native to Canaan as they were practiced already in the Middle Bronze Age, and continue in use through the Late Bronze Age. Furthermore, there is no apparent distinction between how men, women, and children were buried, with all burials showing the same type of grave goods, including pottery, jewelry, weaponry, and other metal objects.[23] One other type of burial practice, which started in the Late Bronze Age, was the use of anthropoid coffins. Showing clear Egyptian influence, the sarcophagi grossly depict the features of a face and hands, obviously lacking the finesse of the Egyptian burials. However, they serve to highlight the impact of Egyptian dominance on almost every aspect of life and death.

The political structure of the ancient Middle East would be completely transformed at the end of the Late Bronze Age around 1200 BCE. The inhabitants of Canaan

21. Kennedy, "A Demographic Analysis of Late Bronze Age Canaan," 99.

22. Gonen, *Burial Patterns & Cultural Diversity in Late Bronze Age Canaan*, 9.

23. Gonen, *Burial Patterns & Cultural Diversity in Late Bronze Age Canaan*, 15.

no longer served Egyptian overlords and smaller local Canaanite kingdoms emerged in the region. However, although the political landscape was changing, much about the aspects of daily life would remain the same. Farming, weaving, food and drink production, and death would continue to dictate the daily lives of the local populations.

3.6 THE END OF THE BRONZE AGE (CA. 1200 BCE)

Around 1200 BCE, the age of international relations that had flourished for a quarter of a millennium during the Late Bronze Age (1550 to 1200 BCE) would come to an end. The Bronze Age collapse was the result of numerous factors. There were possible widespread famines and droughts, which forced empires to fold. Textual sources from Hatti speak of possible famine and grain shortages,[24] however, it unclear whether such shortages were the result of droughts or if this was the result of disruptions to trade routes preventing the import of sufficient supplies. A likely source for such disruptions to trade came at the hands of the Sea Peoples, a conglomeration of roughly nine different tribal groups hailing from Asia Minor to Greece, and perhaps even further in the Mediterranean, who came to the Middle East in search of land and resources. These Sea Peoples brought with them significant advances in technology, including iron weaponry and seafaring skills, which made them a force to be reckoned with in the Middle East.

We learn about the infiltration of these Sea Peoples from several textual sources at the end of the Late Bronze Age. Letters from the final days of Ugarit, which was abandoned and burned in 1185 BCE, tell of the impending doom

24. Bryce, *The Kingdom of the Hittites*, 322, 341.

of the city as the result of attacks from the sea.[25] The best source for understanding the infiltration of the Sea Peoples comes from the Egyptian textual sources at the end of the Late Bronze Age. The Medinet Habu mortuary temple of Rameses III records a long scene depicting nine tribes of the Sea Peoples attacking Egypt. While it appears from the inscription that Egypt was able to fend off the attack in the Egyptian heartland, they lost control of Canaan, and the New Kingdom was significantly weakened.

One of the most famous tribes of the Sea Peoples was the *Peleset,* a name found in the Medinet Habu inscription. Scholars have connected the *Peleset* from the Egyptian sources with the Philistines who settled the coastal area of the southern Levant in the Iron IA period. Assaf Yasur–Landau has argued convincingly for the Aegean origin of this Philistine tribal group, which moved into the land of Canaan.[26]

Whether famine, drought, or Sea People incursions were primarily to blame, the Bronze Age Levant would witness an almost complete collapse around 1200 BCE. The great kingdoms of Hatti, Ugarit, and Egypt would be completely wiped out or significantly weakened. This left a large political vacuum in the land of Canaan, which had been ruled by an iron rod for the previous quarter of a millennium. These Canaanite tribal groups would recognize their opportunity to take power, and groups such as the Israelites and Moabites would reemerge to take back autonomous control.

25. RS 19.011:3–13 (KTU 2.61): "When the messenger arrived, he struck down the watchman, and plundered the city. The food from the threshing floors he burned, and ruined the wines. Our city is ruined. You must surely know!"

26. Yasur-Landau, *The Philistines and Aegean Migration at the End of the Late Bronze Age.*

4

CANAANITES IN THE IRON AGE

4.1 INTRODUCTION

THE CANAANITES FEATURED PROMINENTLY throughout the biblical narratives of the Pentateuch and Joshua, as well as in the first chapters of the book of Judges, serving as the foil for the emerging nation of Israel. Then, seemingly abruptly, references to the Canaanites all but disappear in the books of Samuel and Kings, as the biblical narrative recounts the early years of the monarchic period in Israel. Without understanding the historical context, this apparent disappearance from the pages of the Hebrew Bible would be both surprising and unexpected. However, from the historical evidence so far reviewed, it becomes clear that while the term "Canaanite" may be absent, the Canaanites themselves are not.

During the Middle Bronze Age, local Canaanite rulers maintained autonomous rule over small territories focused around large, walled, urban centers. Then, in the Late Bronze Age, Egyptian control of Canaan significantly curtailed the political autonomy of these rulers, while still allowing Canaanite culture, religion, and language to flourish. These groups, who had been referred to as "Canaanites" by the surrounding populations, had maintained their local ethnic identities and affiliations. Following the collapse of the Bronze Age Levant at the hands of the Sea Peoples, these local tribal groups once again took advantage of the power vacuum by reasserting their autonomy and control. The Canaanite tribal groups from the Bronze Age, who had resided in Canaan for centuries, emerged in the Iron Age as localized kingdoms, including the Phoenicians, Israelites, Moabites, Ammonites, and Edomites. Local textual sources as well as archaeological evidence from the southern Levant provide valuable insight into the development and expansion of each of these groups, as they grew to fill the vacuum created by the Sea Peoples. Even though the term "Canaanite" may not be mentioned in the books of Samuel and Kings, certainly their descendants are the focal point of the biblical narrative.

4.2 IRON AGE I (1200 TO 950 BCE)

While the book of Judges begins with the Israelites facing their Canaanite enemies,[1] the book of 1 Samuel sees the rise of a new enemy. After a brief interlude regarding the priesthood, the fourth chapter of 1 Samuel opens with Israel battling against the Philistines: "The word of Samuel

---

1. Judg 1:1—"After the death of Joshua, the sons of Israel asked of YHWH saying, 'who shall go up for us at first against the Canaanite to do battle with them?'"

came to all of Israel and Israel went out to meet the Philistines in battle" (1 Sam. 4:1). The Philistines—or *Peleset*, as they were known in the Egyptian textual sources of the New Kingdom—were one of the nine groups of the Sea Peoples who were, at least in part, responsible for the fall of the Bronze Age Levant. After severely weakening Egypt, the Philistines saw their opening to move into the fertile region of Canaan. The archaeological record reflects that the Philistines primarily settled the coastal territory of the land of Canaan, especially five cities often referred to as the Philistine Pentapolis: Ashdod, Ekron, Gath, Ashkelon, and Gaza.[2] Lawrence Stager has shown that from 1185 to 1050 BCE, the Philistines continued to expand their territory, taking control of much of the coastal plain, and moving into the Shephelah,[3] as shown in Figure 4.1.

2. Yasur-Landau, *The Philistines and Aegean Migration at the End of the Late Bronze Age*, 282–84. See Yasur-Landau for a discussion of the historicity of the Philistine Pentapolis.

3. Stager, "The Impact of the Sea Peoples in Canaan (1185–1050 BCE)."

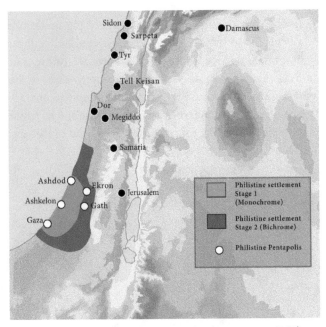

Figure 4.1: Map of Philistine expansion (1185 to 1050 BCE)
Map created by Dillon Paige

While the Philistines moved to take over the coastal plain, another tribal group was expanding to fill the hill country of the Cisjordan. Over the course of the Iron Age I, more than 250 sites cropped up in the hill country, a number that doubled in the Iron Age II.[4] The majority of these Iron Age settlements display a high degree of homogeneity in the material culture: humble four-room pillared houses, stone silos for grain storage, plain pottery such as the collared-rim store jar, and animal bones of ovicaprids (sheep and goats), donkeys, and cattle.[5] Noticeably, pig bones were

4. Finkelstein, "When and How Did the Israelites Emerge?" 80.

5. Dever, *Who Were the Early Israelites and Where Did They Come From?* See chapter 7 for a complete discussion of the material

not found in these settlements, contrasting sharply with the Philistine sites of the coastal plain, where pig bones are prevalent. These remains speak of relatively humble local communities, who engaged in subsistence farming and herding. Many of these settlement features, such as the four-room pillared house style, would continue to characterize settlements in the land of Canaan for several hundred years under the Babylonian invasion at the end of the seventh century.

Figure 4.2: Remains of a four-room house from Area G, City of David, Jerusalem
Photo courtesy of Todd Bolen, BiblePlaces.com

assemblage of the Iron Age I settlements in the hill country of the southern Levant.

Figure 4.3: Reconstruction of a four-room house,
Harvard Semitic Museum
Photo courtesy of Todd Bolen, BiblePlaces.com

Much research has been devoted to identifying the ethnic affiliation of these homogeneous settlements of the hill country of Canaan. Since these settlements were rooted in the Late Bronze Age, but also continued in use throughout the Iron Age, it is likely that these settlers were both Canaanites *and* Israelites. These settlements arose out of the previous Bronze Age Canaanite culture, which is displayed in both their Canaanite language[6] and religion, a topic that will be discussed in more detail below. But there is extra-biblical evidence that supports the conclusion that Israel was already a recognized tribal group by the end of the Late Bronze Age. The Merneptah Victory Stele, discovered at the site of Thebes, was scribed in 1208 BCE and records the conquests of the New Kingdom Pharaoh Merneptah. Like the pharaohs before him, who had frequently made military

6. From a linguistic perspective, Hebrew is classified as part of the Canaanite language family, including also Phoenician/Punic, Moabite, Ammonite, Edomite, and Amarna Canaanite.

conquests, Merneptah records his own exploits in the land of Canaan: "Canaan is captive with all woe. Ashkelon is conquered, Gezer seized, Yanoam made nonexistent; Israel is wasted, bare of seed . . ." (Merneptah Stela: lines 27–28).[7] This early reference may indicate that a tribe of Israel had emerged as a distinct ethnic tribal group in the region of Canaan during the tumultuous transition between the Late Bronze and Iron Age I periods.[8]

This conclusion is supported by the appearance of several other Iron Age kingdoms in the Egyptian sources at the end of the Late Bronze Age. As will be discussed below, Moab was first mentioned under the reign of Ramesses II ca. 1285 BCE,[9] and Edom is also mentioned during the reign of Merneptah ca. 1216 BCE.[10] These early references to Israel, Moab, and Edom suggest that as Egypt was weakening due to attacks by the Sea Peoples, the individual city-states of the Late Bronze Age were uniting and growing more emboldened, resulting in rebellion and reconquest by the pharaohs of the nineteenth dynasty.

This brief historical context provides clarity as to why the Canaanites are not mentioned in the books of Samuel and Kings, and also gives evidence for the emergence of Israel in the landscape of Bronze Age Canaan. The Israelites were themselves part of the Canaanite tradition, having emerged out of the Late Bronze Age culture, retaining their Canaanite culture, religion, and language. Their new foil was the Philistines, who were the newcomers to the

---

7. Lichtheim, "The Poetical Stela of Merneptah (Israel Stela)."

8. Faust, *Israel's Ethnogenesis*, 168–69.

9. Weippert, "The Israelite 'Conquest' and the Evidence from Transjordan," 27.

10. Weippert, "The Israelite "Conquest" and the Evidence from Transjordan," 27.

political stage of the Iron Age I, migrating to the land of Canaan from the Mediterranean region.

Due to the prominence of the Hebrew Bible, we are more familiar with the narrative of ancient Israel, however Israel was not the only Canaanite tribe from the Late Bronze Age that would coalesce and establish its own unique ethnic identity during the Iron Age. The history of the Canaanites in the Iron Age is no longer the history of a single group, but rather the history of a number of tribal groups that formed their own kingdoms. Like the Canaanites of the Bronze Age, who never used that terminology to refer to themselves, there is no textual source that proves that Israel, Moab, Ammon, Edom, and Phoenicia were the descendants of the Bronze Age Canaanites. Rather, the inference is made based upon several key pieces of evidences. First, their emergence at the end of the Late Bronze Age, as described above. Second, that all these groups retained the language of their forbearers, Canaanite, and third, that these populations retained elements of their Canaanite religious culture. It is to these two points that we now turn.

4.2.1 The Rise of Local Canaanite Vernaculars

The earliest example of the Canaanite languages is Amarna Canaanite, which appeared in the Late Bronze Age in the Amarna Letters. Over the next four hundred years this language would evolve, as pronunciations changed, words were borrowed, and morphology developed or decayed as local populations developed their own dialect of Canaanite. By the start of the Iron Age II in 950 BCE, the Canaanite languages of the southern Levant were characterized by increasing linguistic diversity. Yet, since they all still featured the shared innovations of the Canaanite language family, Comparative Semitists classify them as "Canaanite."[11]

Part of the reason we know so much more about these languages and history of these local Canaanite kingdoms is due to the development of a local written vernacular for these groups. In the Iron Age II–III period, the land of Canaan witnessed the emergence of local languages, and local writing systems. Rather than showing obeisance to Egyptian overlords, local kings declared their own great deeds as they sought to establish their kingdoms. In *The Invention of Hebrew*, Seth Sanders describes the emergence of local Canaanite vernaculars in this way: "vernaculars began by pirating the voice of an empire to let a local king speak in a local language, in an attempt to convince an emerging audience that the king's voice was theirs."[12] To exemplify this change, compare the text of an Amarna letter from a Canaanite ruler to Egypt from the Late Bronze Age, with the text of the Moabite Stone written by Mesha', the king of Moab.

---

11. Huehnergard, "Remarks on the Classification of the Northwest Semitic Languages," 285–86. For the sake of clarity, there are four innovative features that characterize all Canaanite languages: 1) the shift of *qattila* and *haqtila* to *qittila* and *hiqtila* in the D- and C-stems, 2) the shift from *'anāku* to *'anōkī*, which evinces the Canaanite shift, 3) the first-person suffix conjugation change from -*tu* to -*ti*, and 4) "the first-person plural marker in Proto-Northwest Semitic was probably -*nū* to mark the subject on the suffix conjugation but -*nā* to mark both the direct object on verbs and the possessive on nouns. Proto-Canaanite saw the generalization of -*nū* in all environments."

12. Sanders, *The Invention of Hebrew*, 154.

El Amarna Letter 320[13] From the ruler of Ashkelon to the pharaoh	Moabite Stone Lines 1–5[14] Written by the Moabite King Mesha'
"[To] the king, my lord, my god, my son, the sun from the sky, . . . I indeed prostrate myself, on the stomach and on the back, at the feet of the king, my lord, seven times and seven times. I am indeed guard[ing] the place of the king where I am. Whatever the k[ing], my lord, has written me, I have listened to very carefully. Who is the dog that would not obey the orders of the king, his lord, the son of the sun?"	"I am Mesha', son of Kemosh[yat], king of Moab, the Dibonite. My father ruled over Moab for thirty years, and I ruled after my father. I made this high place for Kemosh, in Karḥoh, a high pl[ace] of salvation, because he (Kemosh) delivered me from all the kings and because he caused me to look down upon all those who hate me, namely Omri, the king of Israel."

Though different genres, when read side by side, these two texts show the marked contrast between the political landscapes of the Late Bronze and Iron Ages. In the Amarna letter, the Canaanite ruler of Ashkelon portrays himself as a "dog" at the feet of his king, the Egyptian pharaoh. He would never presume to call himself a king or to disobey an order, for fear of retribution. In the Moabite Stone, which is written in Moabite and would have been displayed publicly, King Mesha' extols his great deeds, his divine right to rule, and his kingly lineage. Through the use of the first-person pronoun "I" spoken in the local vernacular of Moab, Mesha' speaks directly to his people, legitimating his rule and uniting his kingdom. Local vernaculars would continue to play an important role in the definition and development of the Canaanite tribal groups of the Iron Age, and it is through

---

13. Moran, *The Amarna Letters*, 350.

14. Translation by author.

these texts that greater insight is gained into their cultural development.

4.2.2 The Continuance of Local Canaanite Religions

Each of the kingdoms of the Iron Age appear to have worshipped a main royal deity, such as Qaus in Edom, Yʜwʜ in Israel, Kemosh in Moab, and Milkom in Ammon. Yet archaeological evidence indicates that the population of the land of Canaan continued to practice their localized expressions of Canaanite religion. As is often the case, though the state may "claim" religion for political purposes, religious practices remain very personal and very integral to the household. Archaeological findings from the Iron Age southern Levant provide ample evidence for some of the core features of these localized religious practices. Entire volumes have been devoted to the topic of Canaanite religion, but for the purposes of this discussion only a cursory overview of some of the core features will be described.

Cultic worship in the southern Levant was typically conducted either in larger public sanctuaries, which served communities and regions, or in local worship areas, which served nuclear or extended families.[15] Larger public sanctuaries included the eighth-century BCE Phoenician temple at Sarepta[16] and the worship complex at the site of Dan, north of the Sea of Galilee, pictured in Figure 4.4 below. These sanctuaries were typically characterized by a large raised altar, often surrounded by an enclosure wall, standing stones, incense burners, and an assortment of other cultic paraphernalia, such as figurines, jewelry, and food

15. Dever, *Did God Have a Wife?* 110–75. Dever provides a detailed overview of the characteristics of both local worship areas and public sanctuaries.

16. Wightman, *Sacred Spaces*, 192

offerings (e.g., animal bones, olive oil). Though the majority of the altar from the site of Dan has not been preserved, excavators uncovered a massive altar foundation nearly five meters or fifteen feet square, along with one of the horns of the altar. With such large cultic installations, these public sanctuaries typically served an entire city or even an entire region, and therefore were large enough to service an entire community as part of a public display of worship.

Figure 4.4: Public sanctuary at the site of Dan
Photo taken by author

Since these public sanctuaries are more spread out in the southern Levant, they were used primarily for larger public events, rather than for private religious practices. For this reason, communities and extended families developed local worship areas for more regular and personal cultic activity. Local worship areas appear to mimic the larger sanctuaries, containing smaller and more poorly crafted standing stones or horned altars such as those pictured in Figure 4.5. These sites also contained other cultic paraphernalia, such as offering stands, jewelry, and dice or astragali (the knucklebones of sheep and goats), which were often used for divination, as seen in Figure 4.6.

Figure 4.5: Incense altars from Megiddo
Photo courtesy of Todd Bolen, BiblePlaces.com

Figure 4.6: Bronze astragalus from Kourion
Photo courtesy of A.D. Riddle, BiblePlaces.com

Certainly these local worship areas would have been an important aspect of daily life in the Iron Age, as individuals or nuclear and extended families gathered to consult with the divine. And while larger public sanctuaries, such as those at Dan or even Jerusalem, would have been significant for regional communal gatherings, their presence did not alter local practices. These religious practices find their origins in the Canaanite Late Bronze Age, and continued to flourish throughout the Iron Age, even as new kingdoms rose up to assert political control.

4.3 THE IRON AGE II–III (950 TO 586 BCE)

For nearly four hundred years, five main kingdoms, Moab, Israel, Ammon, Phoenicia, and Edom, ruled contiguous kingdoms blanketing the land of Canaan. Each of these kingdoms developed a distinctive ethnic identity, complete with a localized religious system, a written vernacular, and a unique material culture. This is not to say that these Iron Age kingdoms ruled unchecked without foreign intervention. After a three-hundred-year period of relative autonomy from the Iron Age I to the beginning of the Iron Age II, the land of Canaan would once again be ruled by a foreign power, Assyria.

4.3.1 Historical Context

The Neo-Assyrian Empire was established in Mesopotamia in 911 BCE in the area of Aššur, and almost immediately dominated the political landscape of the Levant. The Neo-Assyrian Empire went through several cyclical phases of strength and weakness, determining the extent of military control of their empire. The growth and development of the kingdoms of Canaan were entirely dependent upon the status of the Neo-Assyrian Empire. During periods of Assyrian strength, the kingdoms of Canaan served as vassals to the empire, offering regular tribute, but during periods of weakness these local kingdoms grew emboldened, refusing to pay tribute and often uniting with other kingdoms to try to throw off the yoke of Neo-Assyrian rule. These periods of rebellion were punctuated by fierce battles as the Assyrian kings once again ventured into Canaan to reestablish their control. For this reason, a brief history of the Neo-Assyrian Empire is necessary to create the historical context for Iron Age Canaan.

Years (BCE)	Phase	Rulers	Significant Events
911 to 824	Phase I: Expansion	Adad-Nirari II Ashurnasirpal II Shalmaneser III	853 BCE—Battle of Qarqar 841 BCE—Jehu of Israel pays tribute to Assyria
824 to 750	Phase II: Weakness	Shamshi-Adad V Adad-Nirari III Shalmaneser IV Ashur-Dan III Adad-Nirari V	806 BCE—Adad-Nirari conquers the Levant, returns to Assyria
750 to 640	Phase III: Conquest & Deportation	Tiglath-Pileser III Shalmaneser V Sargon II Sennacherib Esarhaddon Ashurbanipal	732 BCE—Tiglath-Pileser besieges Samaria 721 BCE—Sargon deports 27,000 inhabitants from Samaria 701 BCE—Sennacherib conquers forty-five cities in Canaan, besieges Jerusalem
640 to 609	Phase IV: Decline & Demise	Ashurbanipal cont. Ashur-etil-ilani Sinsharishkun Ashur-uballit II	612 BCE—Fall of Nineveh 609 BCE—Battle of Haran

Figure 4.7: Timeline of the Neo-Assyrian Empire

The first king of the empire, Adad-Nirari II (911 to 891 BCE), embarked on military campaigns throughout much of the known world, sweeping through the land of Canaan as well, establishing the vast Neo-Assyria Empire.

This set a pattern for subsequent kings, since military conquests were an essential part of their rule. This strong military rule would be continued by the next two successive kings Ashurnasirpal II, and Shalmaneser III, who similarly maintained political control over the land of Canaan.

However, following the end of the reign of Shalmaneser III, for the seventy-five-year period from 824 to 750 BCE, a period of greater independence was enjoyed by the small kingdoms in Canaan, allowing the Canaanite rulers to once again grow bold. Shalmaneser's successor Shamshi-Adad V (823 to 811 BCE) certainly "portrayed himself as a victorious warrior, however the dominance over Syria had disappeared and states there refused to pay tribute."[17] This pattern persisted as the Assyrian Empire continued to weaken, and "in the first half of the eighth century Assyria had lost its ability to campaign outside its borders, and internally local officials had usurped some of the royal powers."[18]

This brief period of independence enjoyed by the kingdoms of Canaan was abruptly cut short by the second wave of Assyrian aggression characterized by a series of strong leaders who greatly expanded the Assyrian territory. This second wave occurred from roughly 750 to 681, corresponding to the Iron Age IIB, during the reigns of Tiglath-Pileser III (744 to 727), Shalmaneser V (726 to 722), Sargon II (721 to 705), Sennacherib (705 to 681), and Ashurbanipal (668 to 640).[19] In seeking to avoid the mistakes of the previous kings, who could not keep rebellion in check, Tiglath-Pileser III and his successors instituted "a policy

17. Mieroop, *A History of the Ancient Near East ca. 3000–323 BC*, 244.

18. Mieroop, *A History of the Ancient Near East*, 248.

19. Gilbert, *Syro-Hittite Monumental Art and the Archaeology of Performance*, 8.

of radical subjugation with ample use of siege warfare and mass deportations,"[20] transplanting Canaanite populations from Canaan to the Assyrian heartland, effectively ending any possibility of future local rebellion.

The final period of the Neo-Assyrian Empire was once again characterized by weakness, as the empire gradually deteriorated and became more insular. The fall of Nineveh, the Assyrian capital, in 612 BCE, and the defeat of the Assyrian troops at the Battle of Haran (609 BCE) effectively marked the end of the Neo-Assyrian Empire at the hands of the Babylonians. During this period, the kingdoms of Canaan once again asserted their political independence. As we sketch the history of the land of Canaan in the Iron Age II–III period, it is important to understand the history of the Assyrian Empire as the framework for the development, expansion, and demise of the five main kingdoms of Canaan.

4.4 KINGDOMS OF CANAAN IN IRON AGE II–III

While there were other smaller tribal groups in the area of the land of Canaan during this period, textual sources reveal the history of five main kingdoms: Moab, Edom, Ammon, Phoenicia, and Israel. All of these kingdoms appear to find their ancestral roots in the Late Bronze Age Canaanite tribal groups, maintaining elements of their Canaanite cultural heritage. All of these groups spoke Canaanite languages and retained elements of Canaanite religion. Though the pantheon of the Late Bronze Age was quite extensive, in the Iron Age most of the kingdoms of Canaan maintained a single royal deity, such as Qaus in Edom, Yhwh in Israel, Kemosh in Moab, and Milkom in Ammon. Whole volumes

20. Gilbert, *Syro-Hittite Monumental Art*, 8.

have been devoted to the history and culture of these kingdoms, but the scope of this volume is far more limited. The cursory review of the kingdoms below is intended as a brief overview of their history, with a focus on how these kingdoms developed out of their Late Bronze Age Canaanite roots.

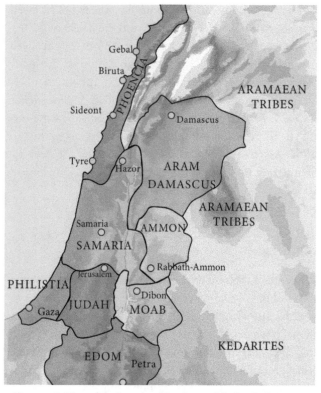

Figure 4.8: Map of the Iron Age kingdoms of the land of Canaan
Map created by Dillon Paige

4.4.1 Edom

Throughout the Late Bronze Age, the region of Edom was mentioned in Egyptian sources as the "mountains of Seir." The political entity of Edom is first mentioned in the Papyrus Anastasi VI, dated to the eighth year of the reign of Merneptah (1216 BCE). "In the papyrus, the Edomites themselves turn out to be nomads, who appear with their herds on the eastern border of Egypt and request permission to use the water holes in the Wadi Tumilat."[21] This early appearance of Edom in Egyptian sources corresponds temporally with the reference to Israel during the reign of Merneptah, and serves to emphasize that the Iron Age kingdoms emerged from the Canaanite tribes of the Late Bronze Age. From this early reference in Egyptian sources, as well as subsequent references in Assyrian sources and the Hebrew Bible, it appears that Edom occupied the territory south of the Dead Sea, straddling the Negev and Nefud Deserts in the modern-day countries of Israel and Jordan.

Very little is known about the Edomite kingdom, due to limited textual sources having been uncovered in Edomite, but it does appear that Edom had a functioning monarchic system, a unique religious system, and a written vernacular. Assyria texts record kings of Edom offering tribute to their Assyrian overlords, like much of the rest of the southern Levantine kingdoms. The first king of Edom mentioned in extra-biblical texts is the king Qaus-malak, who is seen giving tribute to the Neo-Assyrian Tiglath-Pilesar, and a later Edomite king Qaus-gabar is seen giving tribute to Esarhaddon in the seventh century.[22] Unlike some of the rebellious kingdoms of the northern Levant,

21. Weippert, "The Israelite 'Conquest' and the Evidence from Transjordan," 27.

22. Millard, "Assyrian Involvement in Edom," 36–37.

Assyria never put Edom under direct rule, instead allowing it to maintain local rule, always referring to the Edomite rulers as "kings."

In addition to the monarchic system, the Edomite kingdom may have developed their own written vernacular. This statement is caveated by the fact that, due to the limited nature of the texts that have been discovered in the Edomite heartland, it is still impossible to identify any unique innovations of Edomite that distinguish it from other Canaanite languages such as Hebrew. However, other scholars have argued that it should be considered its own local corpus based upon stylistic features of the Edomite script.[23] These texts also include some evidence regarding the chief deity of the Edomites, Qaus (*qws*), who is regularly included in blessing formulae. Edom falls out of the historical sources, and some suggest their descendants can be traced to the future Idumaeans, though this is far from certain.

4.4.2 Moab

Similar to Israel and Edom, Moab first appears in the Egyptian textual sources at the end of the Late Bronze Age. Moab is first mentioned early in the reign of Ramesses II, about 1285 BCE. The reference to Moab appears "in the representation of a fortress which Ramesses II had ordered drawn on the East Wall of his court in the Luxor Temple: 'the town which the mighty arm of Pharaoh plundered in the Land of Moab.'"[24] Already by the beginning of the thirteenth century, Moab was a distinct geopolitical entity which Egypt conquered as part of its regular campaigns into Canaan.

23. Vanderhooft, "The Edomite Dialect and Script."

24. Weippert, "The Israelite 'Conquest' and the Evidence from Transjordan," 27.

Due to a paucity of textual sources, little is known about Moab until ca. 840 BCE, the date of the Moabite Stone discussed above. Since this inscription is quite long, a great deal of information is gained about the royal lineage, the religious pantheon, Moabite relations with other kingdoms, and the linguistic orientation of Moabite. First, the Moabite royal lineage was hereditary, being passed from father to son, and the rulers described themselves as "kings" reigning over the land of Moab. The text also mentions the chief deity of Moab, Kemosh. Though the Moabite pantheon was likely much broader, the chief deity of Moab, Kemosh, is regularly mentioned in texts as being the source of Moabite power. Finally, Mesha' also complains about relations with Israel across the Jordan River, saying that king Omri of Israel had formerly oppressed Moab, but that in his reign he achieved retribution by subduing the "house of David." Since the text is so long, there is sufficient linguistic evidence to describe Moabite as its own distinct language, yet still a part of the Canaanite language family.

Figure 4.9: Moabite stone on display in the Louvre Museum
Photo courtesy of Todd Bolen, BiblePlaces.com

Moab benefitted economically under Assyrian rule, and from trade with other kingdoms in the region, while still retaining its own ethnic identity. Daviau has argued that during the eighth and seventh centuries, there existed "increased trade and exchange along the north–south corridor between Edom and the Assyrian provinces," a trade that "may have been directly related to expanding Assyrian influence and control in the region."[25] Moab's access to lucrative trade was likely due to its important control over the

25. Dion and Daviau, "The Moabites," 224.

King's Highway, a main trade route between Assyria and Egypt. Moab continued to prosper under Assyrian rule but was attacked and subjugated under the following Babylonian Empire, and eventually disappeared from historical sources.

4.4.3 Ammon

Unlike Moab, Edom, and Israel, which were mentioned in Egyptian sources from the end of the Late Bronze Age, there is no reference to Ammon until the Assyrian period. The early history of Ammon is also difficult to ascertain from archaeological sources as there is still an incomplete picture as to the territory of the Ammonites in the Iron Age. Daviau, in her work on the excavations of Tell Jawa, stated that "there is no doubt whatsoever that the Ammonite capital Rabbah was located at present-day Amman, more precisely on the Amman citadel. Unfortunately Rabbah, the capital, is the only ancient toponym that can be located with reasonable certainty,"[26] making it difficult to delineate the entire territory of Ammon.

The first possible reference to Ammon is to king "Baasha son of Ruḫub of the land of Ammon/Aman" in the Kurkh Monolith, which records the Battle of Qarqar in 853 BCE, but this reference is uncertain. The first sure reference comes during the reign of Tiglath-Pilesar III's campaign through Canaan in 734 BCE.[27] Along with the kings of Moab and Edom, Šanip of the house of Ammon offers tribute to Tiglath Pilesar. In the eighth century, Ammonite rulers were not described as "kings" by Assyrian sources, but this shifts in the seventh century, where we find "Pado'il king of the house of Ammon" under Esarhaddon

26. Daviau, *Excavations at Tall Jawa, Jordan*, 485–89.

27. Tyson, *The Ammonites*, 72–75.

(680 to 669 BCE) and "Amminadab king of the house of Ammon" under Assurbanipal (668 to 627 BCE). Though there is little evidence for the relationship between Ammon and Assyria, it is possible that this shift in designation may indicate that "as a vassal Ammon provided material support to the Neo-Assyrian forces in the form of food, manpower, and intelligence."[28] Ammon similarly fared well during the Babylonian period, and there is evidence that Ammon continued to exist through the Greek and Roman periods. From Jewish sources, the Ammonites are attested joining with other local tribes to oppose the rise of Judas Maccabaeus ca. 167 BCE (1 Macc 5:6).

Similar to the other Iron Age kingdoms of Canaan, Ammon developed its own written vernacular. There are 274 total texts written in Ammonite, which have been preserved on stone, metal, pottery, bullae, bone, and gem stones.[29] From these inscriptions roughly eighty-five nouns and seventy-five verbs are reconstructed, many of which are attested only in personal names.[30] From these texts information is preserved regarding the Ammonite pantheon, and the two most common deities are El, a common Canaanite deity, and Milkom, who was either a distinct deity or a royal form of the god El.[31]

4.4.4 Israel and Judah

Certainly the most famous kingdom in the land of Canaan is that of Israel, later divided into the northern tribes of Samaria/Israel, and the southern tribes of Judah. The books of 1 & 2 Samuel, 1 & 2 Kings, and 1 & 2 Chronicles deal with

---

28. Tyson, *The Ammonites*, 76.

29. Aufrecht, "Ammonite Texts and Language," 164.

30. Aufrecht, "Ammonite Texts and Language," 175–77.

31. Tyson, *The Ammonites*, 228.

the history of Israel and Judah during this period, not to mention several books from the Writings and the Prophets that deal with this time period. Entire volumes have been dedicated to the history of Israel and Judah from both texts and artifacts, but for the purposes of this volume, only a cursory overview of Israelite history and culture will be reviewed as an extension of the Canaanite culture of the Late Bronze Age.

The humble and rural settlements of the Iron Age I discussed above coalesced during the Iron Age II–III into the formation of the kingdom of Israel, whose influence was felt throughout the ancient Middle East. In the second half of the tenth century, a discernible change is observed in the archaeological record as large urban centers characterized by palatial architecture, casemate fortification systems, and multi-chambered gates emerge at sites throughout Israel, such as Khirbet Qeiyafa, Hazor, and Megiddo.[32] Some scholars have linked the development of these large public building works with the emergence of the first Israelite monarchy as related in the biblical narrative, a perspective that may be strengthened by the mention of the "house of David" (*bytdwd*) in the Aramaic stele found at Tel Dan.[33]

More concrete evidence for the emergence of northern Israel is found in the first half of the ninth century, when the Omride dynasty, centered at the northern city of Samaria,[34] would surface as a prominent political entity. The Moabite Mesha' inscription recounts the military

32. Barkay, "Iron II–III."

33. Mazar, "The Search for David and Solomon: An Archaeological Perspective."

34. The capital of the northern kingdom, Samaria, would grow in size and grandeur during this period, with the construction of a large two-tiered, enclosed palace complex complete with Phoenician-style ivories.

exploits of King Omri, who campaigned throughout the territory of Moab in modern-day Jordan.[35] The Assyrian Kurkh relief notes that king "Ahab, the Israelite, mustered 10,000 chariots" to join forces at the Battle of Qarqar in 853 BCE against the Assyrian King Shalmaneser III. These external sources suggest that the northern Israelite kings, Omri and Ahab, possessed the military resources to play a prominent political role in this period. Yet ultimately, the small northern territory of Israel was no match for the growing might of the Neo-Assyrian Empire, and the Assyrian inscription known as the Black Obelisk, constructed in the second half of the reign of Shalmaneser III, pictures "Jehu of the house of Omri" groveling at the feet of the mighty Assyrian king when offering tribute.[36]

Assyria continued to expand its territory in the southern Levant, bringing about the complete destruction of the once prominent city of Samaria at the hands of Sargon II ca. 720 BCE. But in a unique twist of history, as the stronger northern territory of Israel would fade from political significance, the weaker, southern kingdom of Judah, retained some degree of autonomy in the face of Assyrian aggression, and would continue to exist for the next hundred and fifty years. Two decades after the fall of Samaria, the Assyrian king, Sennacherib, swept through the southern Levant, destroying key fortified cities such as Lachish in 701 BCE,[37]

35. Aḥituv, *Echoes from the Past*, 390–91.

36. Miller and Hayes, *A History of Ancient Israel and Judah*. Chapters 8 and 9 of this volume provide perhaps the best overview of the relevant Assyrian and Egyptian textual sources for reconstructing the early history of Israel.

37. The Lachish reliefs found in the throne room of Sennacherib at Kuyunjik (Nineveh) as well as the Sennacherib Prism record the impressive conquest of the southern Levant at the hands of Assyria at the end of the eighth century. Excavations at the site of Lachish have yielded a destruction layer dating roughly to 701 BCE, along with a

but failed to conquer Jerusalem, perhaps due to increased defensive construction as recorded in the Siloam Tunnel inscription.[38] The preservation of the capital city of Jerusalem allowed the small kingdom of Judah to continue as a vassal of the Assyrian Empire for the next century.

Archaeological evidence from the period records the great impact that Assyrian dominance had on the region.[39] Strategically-placed Assyrian administrative centers, such as the one found at Megiddo Stratum III, maintained military control of the region and ensured the steady flow of tribute from Judah to the Assyrian heartland. Settlement patterns indicate that large portions of the population were moved away from rural villages into large urban centers, such as Jerusalem and Ekron, likely to facilitate Assyrian military control.

As Assyria weakened in the second half of the seventh century under pressure from the newly emerging Neo-Babylonian Empire, Judah again experienced a period of autonomy. Sites that had long been abandoned, such as Lachish, were refortified, and a wealth of epigraphic material—such as the ostraca (inked pottery sherds) found at the sites of Lachish, Arad, and Masad Hashavyahu (Yavneh Yam)—provide important information as to the administrative system that emerged in the wake of Assyrian control. The Lachish letters refer to the movements of troops (Lachish 3) and the Arad ostraca refer to the distribution of rations (Arad Ostracon 18), suggesting that Judah operated as an independent political entity toward the end of the seventh century.[40] Furthermore, these ostraca were writ-

---

large Assyrian siege ramp, which was used to conquer the city.

38. Aḥituv, *Echoes from the Past*, 19–25.

39. Stern, *Archaeology of the Land of the Bible 2, 732–332 BCE*, 3–41.

40. Aḥituv, *Echoes from the Past*, 62–69, 119–21.

ten in Hebrew and were distributed to sites throughout the southern Levant, making it clear that native scribes, writing in the local vernacular, were in place throughout the kingdom of Judah. Unfortunately, as with the Omride dynasty of the ninth century, this period of Judean hegemony was short-lived, lasting roughly half a century, until the city of Jerusalem was destroyed in 586 BCE by Nebuchadnezzar, the king of the Neo-Babylonian Empire.[41]

4.4.5 Phoenicia

The history of Phoenicia goes back well into the third millennium, as the territory controlled key ports, affording it a major trade role in the ancient world. Sites such as Byblos (*Gubla*), Tyre (*Ṣurru*), Beirut (*Biruta*), and Sidon (*Ṣiduna*) all appear in the Amarna letters controlled by local Canaanite rulers. Like the rest of the southern Levant, the Phoenician coast underwent a period of obscurity through the Iron Age I, with little political activity, and it was not until the Iron Age II–III that the Phoenician city-states once again returned to power.

In fact, the notion of a greater Phoenician kingdom, did not exist in the ancient world. The terms "*Phoinikes* for the people and *Phoinike* for the region" were a later Greek invention used to refer to the coastal populations. The terminology is found as early as the writings of Homer, but was never adopted by the people themselves.[42] Rather, in inscriptions there are two primarily ethnic or political terms used. First, the Phoenician city-states often referred to themselves as "Canaanites" and to their land as "Canaan," such that "the correct and original name of the Phoenicians

41. The early years of the Babylonian Empire are preserved in detail in the Babylonian Chronicle.

42. Moscati, *The Phoenicians*, 24.

was Canaanites."[43] Second, and more common, the Phoenician populations associated themselves with their local independent city-state of the Phoenician coast. The strength of these local states meant that "the concept of national unity was hazy among the Phoenician cities."[44] This lack of national unity was certainly due in part to the topography of the Phoenician coast, which was chopped up by rivers flowing from the mountain range creating a series of disconnected valleys.

Due to their proximity to ports, the Phoenicians were well known for their seafaring prowess, and this caused them to receive preferential treatment from empires. In the ninth century, Phoenicia, like the rest of the kingdoms of Canaan, paid tribute to the Assyrian rulers. However, under Tiglath-Pilesar III they reached a new level of prosperity as they became the center of shipping trade for Assyria, something that would be repeated in the Persian period.

Like the other kingdoms of Canaan, the Phoenician city-states developed a local written vernacular, Phoenician and later Punic, both of which are Canaanite languages. In fact, the Phoenicians were responsible for developing the alphabet and script that was borrowed by the other Canaanite kingdoms as well as by the Aramaeans, and eventually, through the pervasive spread of Aramaic during the Persian Empire, it evolved into the Arabic script. This original Phoenician alphabet was also the source of the Latin alphabet. In around the eighth century BCE, through interaction with the Phoenician city-states, the Greeks borrowed the Phoenician script to transcribe Greek. Since the Semitic languages record only consonants, the Greeks subsequently adapted the scripts and order of the letters to

---

43. Aubet, *The Phoenicians and the West*, 9–11.

44. Moscati, *The Phoenicians*, 24.

support their language with vowels, and it is this alphabet that was later borrowed by the Romans to transcribe Latin.

Unlike Moabite, Edomite, and Ammonite, which are poorly attested, the Phoenician and Punic corpora are quite well attested in several thousand texts. Also, like the other kingdoms of Canaan, it appears that each city-state associated itself with specific royal deities; in Byblos, the god El and the goddess Baalat, in Sidon, Baal and Ashtart, and in Tyre, the god Melqart. Other deities were certainly worshipped, but were likely less significant.

It is in Phoenicia that the Canaanites find their final legacy. As other Canaanite kingdoms would eventually disappear from history or disassociate themselves from their previous Canaanite lineage, the Phoenicians would continue to see themselves as Canaanites. The next chapter will discuss this legacy in more detail.

5

THE LEGACY
OF THE CANAANITES

THE FALL OF NINEVEH in 612 BCE and the Assyrian loss at the Battle of Haran in 609 BCE marked the end of the Neo-Assyrian Empire, ushering in the Babylonian Empire. For roughly seventy years, the land of Canaan was sparsely inhabited, until the rise of the Persian Empire that ruled from Elam. Over the next several millennia, the land of Canaan continued to be ruled by major empires, including the Persian Empire, the Greek Empire, the Roman Empire, the Byzantine Empire, and the Arab Caliphates. The kingdoms of Moab, Edom, and Ammon gradually disappeared from history sustaining little connection to their Late Bronze Age Canaanite roots. As is well known, much of the nation of Israel was deported to Babylon in 586 BCE and returned in part under the Persian Empire. Though Israel may have emerged out of the Late Bronze Age context, the biblical narratives would strictly distinguish Israel from its Canaanite neighbors. Only in Phoenicia does the legacy of the Canaanites continue for almost another millennium.

5.1 THE PHOENICIANS: THE HISTORIC LEGACY OF THE CANAANITES

Like much of the rest of the land of Canaan, the Phoenician city-states were destroyed by Babylon, and were left virtually uninhabited for roughly seventy years. Ephraim Stern, who has been the main excavator at the Phoenician site of Dor, described this tumultuous period: "when the Babylonian army first came to this region, it laid a lengthy siege against Tyre and some other Phoenician cities until they were conquered and destroyed," and all the sites from the region such as Acco, Dor, Jaffa, and Tell Keisan reflect this Babylonian destruction, with a clear occupation gap extending until the resettlement in the Persian period.[1]

The Phoenician city-states witnessed a great deal of economic growth and autonomy under Achaemenid rule. Individual city-states minted their own coinage, had independent weights and measures, and maintained their own dynastic lines, all within the overarching sovereignty of the Persian Empire.[2] Phoenician city-states continued to flourish in the Persian period, in part due to their prominence in the Persian military. Phoenician ships formed the main component of the Persian fleet as attested by the fact that "Darius used them for his war with the Ionian Greeks and in Xerxes' fleet at Salamis (480 BCE) there were 300 Phoenician triremes out of a total of 1,207."[3] In return for this

1. Stern, *Archaeology of the Land of the Bible 2, 732–332 BCE*, 315–16.

2. Acquaro, "Coins," 464.

3. Harden, *The Phoenicians*, 125.

military service, "the Phoenicians were treated particularly well, granted a great degree of freedom and the financial demands upon them were moderate."[4]

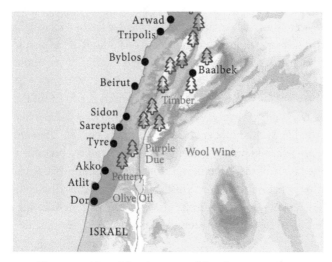

Figure 5.1: Map of the city-states of the Phoenician Coast
Map created by Dillon Paige

This prosperity did not continue in the Greek and Roman periods. As part of his conquest of the Middle East, Alexander the Great conquered the region, bringing it under Greek rule. The Phoenician city-states fell under the control of subsequent rules until eventually they were incorporated into the Roman Empire. In the Greek and Roman periods, though Phoenicia essentially lost their autonomous control, they still played an important role in international trade due to the production of one key luxury trade good, namely the purple dyed cloth, sometimes known as "Tyrian purple." The purple color was produced by either milking or crushing the murex sea snails found exclusively in

4. Massa, *The Phoenicians*, 50.

the eastern portion of the Mediterranean Sea. As early as the Late Bronze Age (ca. 1550 to 1200 BCE), Phoenicians were known for mass producing and trading cloth dyed in shades of purple, red, and blue. So valuable was the dyed cloth that in the Greek period purple dye fetched its weight in silver[5] and in the Roman period, one pound of the purple dye cost roughly three pounds of gold (equivalent to about $19,000 today).[6]

It is in the Greek and Roman periods that we find the last textual references to the Canaanites. Philo of Byblos, who lived in the first century CE, recalls a person *Chanaan* who was rebaptized under the name *Phoinix,* becoming the father of the Phoenicians,[7] offering a pseudo-historical interpretation for the origins of the Phoenicians. The New Testament also closely links Phoenicians with the Canaanites. Matthew 15:22 recounts the story of a woman described as a "Canaanite" (Χαναναία), indicating she hailed from the region of Canaan. The parallel passage in Mark 7:26 records this same woman as being from the region of Syro-Phoenicia (Συροφοινίκισσα), showing that the region of the southern Levant was still equated with Canaan in the Roman period.

The latest textual reference to the Canaanites comes from the writings of Saint Augustine in his *Epistulae ad Romanos* 13, where the term is used to describe either the population residing in Phoenician North Africa or to the language they were speaking.[8] Whatever the referent, the

5. Athenaeus, *The Deipnosophists*. Theopompus cited by Athenaeus (12:526).

6 Graser, "A Text and Translation of the Edict of Diocletian."

7. Aubet, *The Phoenicians and the West*, 9–11.

8. Quinn, McLynn, Kerr, and Hadas, "Augustine's Canaanites," 176–77. See notes 4 and 5 for a discussion of all other possible references to Canaan or Canaanites in late sources. Quinn et al. argue that

term "Canaanite" was still being used in this late period more than two millennia after the first citation, back in the Middle Bronze Age.

The lack of textual references to the Canaanites in the region of Phoenicia does not necessarily mean that the Canaanites had disappeared. Recent genetic research has shown that the Phoenicians, who descended from the Canaanites, continued to reside in the region of the Phoenician coast for another two millennia. The genetic study, which connected the residents of the Early Bronze Age site of 'Ain Ghazal in Jordan with the inhabitants of Middle Bronze Age Sidon, also tested samples from the modern-day population of Lebanon.[9] The team sequenced the genomes of ninety-nine residents of Lebanon and compared these findings with the genetic data from ancient Sidon. The consistency between the two data sets shows convincing proof for genetic continuity from 1600 BCE to the present. The researchers noted that "present-day Lebanese derive most of their ancestry from a Canaanite-related population, which therefore implies substantial genetic continuity in the Levant since at least the Bronze Age."[10] Though the final textual reference to the Canaanites is from the fourth century CE, these new findings provide a degree of support for the continued flourishing of the Canaanite population until the present day.

---

the use of the term "Canaanite" in Augustine's letter does not refer to the ethnic identity of the people, but rather is used to describe their language. In either case, it is significant that the term "Canaanite" is still being used to refer either to a language or a people at such a late period.

9. Haber, et al., "Continuity and Admixture in the Last Five Millennia of Levantine History," 277.

10. Haber, et al., "Continuity and Admixture in the Last Five Millennia of Levantine History," 274.

5.2 THE HEBREW BIBLE: THE LITERARY LEGACY OF THE CANAANITES

While the Canaanites may find their genetic lineage in the present-day Phoenician coastlines of Lebanon, their linguistic and literary legacy is found in the Hebrew Bible. Out of the six languages that historically comprised the Canaanite language family—Phoenician/Punic, Edomite, Moabite, Ammonite, Amarna Canaanite, and Hebrew—all are now extinct, except for Hebrew, which has been resurrected in the form of Modern Hebrew spoken in Israel. While the language of Modern Hebrew has certainly undergone numerous changes over the last several millennia, it is still linguistically descended from Proto-Canaanite, likely active in the Bronze Age.

Even though the Amarna letters of the Late Bronze Age, as well as the corpora of the Iron Age kingdoms of the land of Canaan preserve in part the literary traditions of the Canaanites, the most well-known corpus discussing the history and identity of the Canaanites is undoubtedly the Hebrew Bible. As discussed, there are over 150 mentions of the terms "Canaan" and "Canaanites" in the Hebrew Bible, and while at times the term is used more generally to refer to the people inhabiting the land of Canaan, in most cases the Canaanites are described as an idolatrous and wicked population deserving of judgment. It is this telling of history that has been preserved for the past three millennia without the aid of archaeology and uncovered textual sources. Certainly this is the predominant view of "Canaanites" in the West, but as will be seen below, there is a push in the modern Middle East to reclaim the terms "Canaan" and "Canaanite" and to use them in the modern political discourse.

5.3 THE MODERN MIDDLE EAST: THE POLITICAL LEGACY OF THE CANAANITES

This volume opened with quotes from two modern Middle Eastern politicians. In each case, the politician deliberately references the terms "Canaan" or "Canaanite" to bolster his political claims. Indeed, the notion of Canaan is integral to the political ideologies of the Middle East. It is for this reason that it is essential to understand the historical origins of the Canaanites, and also to understand the medium through which these perspectives are being refracted. Rather than assigning value or accuracy to either of these claims, the purpose in including these here is simply to show the significant impact that ancient history can have on modern culture. Though the massive Bronze Age fortifications of the Canaanites have disappeared, the Canaanite legacy continues today.

BIBLIOGRAPHY

Acquaro, E. "Coins." In *The Phoenicians*, edited by S. Moscati, 464–73. Milan: Bompiani, 1988.

Aḥituv, S. *Echoes from the Past: Hebrew and Cognate Inscriptions from the Biblical Period*. Jerusalem: Carta, 2008.

Arnold, B. T., and B. E. Beyer. *Encountering the Old Testament: A Christian Survey*. 3rd ed. Grand Rapids: Baker, 2015.

Astour, M. C. "The Origin of the Terms 'Canaan,' 'Phoenician,' and 'Purple.'" *Journal of Near Eastern Studies* 24 (1965) 346–50.

Athenaeus. *The Deipnosophists*. Translated by C. B. Gulick. Cambridge: Harvard University Press, 1941.

Aubet, M. E. *The Phoenicians and the West*. 2nd ed. New York: Cambridge University Press, 2001.

Aufrecht, W. E. "Ammonite Texts and Language." In *Ancient Ammon*, edited by B. MacDonald and R. Younker, 163–88. Studies in the History and Culture of the Ancient Near East XVII. Leiden: Brill, 1999.

Barkay, G. "Iron II–III." In *The Archaeology of Ancient Israel*, edited by A. Ben-Tor, 302–73. New Haven: Yale University Press, 1992.

Bimson, J. J. *Redating the Exodus and Conquest*. Sheffield, UK: Journal for the Study of the Old Testament, 1978.

Brovarsky, E., S. K. Doll, R. Freed. *Egypt's Golden Age: The Art of Living in the New Kingdom 1558–1085 B.C.* Boston: Museum of Fine Arts, 1982.

Bryce, T. R. *The Kingdom of the Hittites*. Oxford: Oxford University Press, 2005.

Buck, M. E. *The Amorite Dynasty of Ugarit: Historical Implications of Linguistic and Archaeological Parallels*. Studies in the Archaeology and History of the Levant 8. Leiden: Brill, 2020.

Burke, A. A. "The Architecture of Defense: Fortified Settlements of the Levant during the Middle Bronze Age." PhD diss., University of Chicago, 2004.

———. *"Walled Up to Heaven": The Evolution of Middle Bronze Age Fortification Strategies in the Levant*. Studies in the Archaeology and History of the Levant 4. Winona Lake, IN: Eisenbrauns, 2008.

Charpin, D., and N. Ziegler. *Mari et le Proche-Orient à l'époque amorrite: Essai d'histoire politique*. Florilegium Marianum 5. Paris: Société pour l'étude du Proche-Orient ancient, 2003.

Clayden, T. "Dūr-Kurigalzu: New Perspectives." In *Karduniaš: Babylonia under the Kassites,* edited by A. Bartelmus and K. Sternitzke, 437–78. Boston: de Gruyter, 2017.

Cohen, S. *Canaanites, Chronologies, and Connections: The Relationship of Middle Bronze IIA Canaan to Middle Kingdom Egypt*. Studies in the Archaeology and History of the Levant 3. Winona Lake, IN: Eisenbrauns, 2002.

———. "Interpretative Uses and Abuses of the Beni Hasan Tomb Painting." *Journal of Near Eastern Studies* 74 (2015) 19–38.

Daviau, P. M. M. *Excavations at Tall Jawa, Jordan: The Iron Age Town*. Leiden: Brill, 2003.

Dever, W. G. *Did God Have a Wife? Archaeology and Folk Religion in Ancient Israel*. Grand Rapids: Eerdmans, 2005.

———. *Who Were the Early Israelites and Where Did They Come From?* Grand Rapids: Eerdmans, 2006.

Dion, P. E., and P. M. M. Daviau. "The Moabites." In *The Books of Kings: Sources, Composition, Historiography, and Reception,* edited by A. Lemaire and B. Halpern, 205–24. Leiden: Brill, 2010.

Dossin, G. "Une mention de Cananéens dans une lettre de Mari." *Syria* 50 (1973) 277–82.

Durand, J. M. *Documents épistolaires du palais de Mari, tome II*. Littératures Anciennes du Proche-Orient 17. Paris: Les Éditions du Cerf, 1998.

———. "Villes fantômes de Syrie et autres lieux." *Mari Annales de Recherches Interdisciplinaires* 7 (1987) 199–234.

Ebeling, J. "Women's Daily Life in Bronze Age Canaan." In *Women in Antiquity: Real Women across the Ancient World,* edited by S. L. Budin and J. M. Turfa, 465–75. London: Routledge, 2016.

Faust, A. *Israel's Ethnogenesis: Settlement, Interaction, Expansion, and Resistance*. London: Equinox, 2006.

Finkelstein, I. "When and How Did the Israelites Emerge?" In *The Quest for the Historical Israel: Debating Archaeology and History of Early Israel. Invited Lectures Delivered at the Sixth Biennial Colloquium of the International Institute for Secular Humanistic Judaism, Detroit, October 2005 by Israel Finkelstein and Amihai Mazar*, edited by B. B. Schmidt, 73–83. Archaeology and Biblical Studies 17. Atlanta: Society of Biblical Literature; Leiden: Brill, 2007.

Garfinkel, Y., S. Ganor, and M. Hasel. *In the Footsteps of King David: Revelations from an Ancient Biblical City*. London: Thames and Hudson, 2018.

Gilbert, A. *Syro-Hittite Monumental Art and the Archaeology of Performance*. Berlin: de Gruyter, 2011.

Gonen, R. *Burial Patterns & Cultural Diversity in Late Bronze Age Canaan*. American Schools of Oriental Research: Dissertation Series 7. Winona Lake, IN: Eisenbrauns, 1992.

Graser, E. R. "A Text and Translation of the Edict of Diocletian." In *An Economic Survey of Ancient Rome Volume V: Rome and Italy of the Empire*, edited by T. Frank, 307–421. Baltimore: Johns Hopkins University Press, 1940.

Greenberg, R., S. Paz, D. Wengrow, and M. Iserlis. "Tel Bet Yerah: Hub of the Early Bronze Age Levant." *Near Eastern Archaeology* 75 (2012) 88–107.

Greener, A. "Archaeology and Religion in Late Bronze Age Canaan." *Religions* 10.258 (2019) 1–17.

Haber, M., C. Doumet-Serhal, C. Scheib, Y. Xue, P. Danecek, et al. "Continuity and Admixture in the Last Five Millennia of Levantine History from Ancient Canaanite and Present-Day Lebanese Genome Sequences." *The American Journal of Human Genetics* 101 (2017) 274–82.

Harden, D. *The Phoenicians*. Ancient Peoples and Places Series 26. London: Thames and Hudson, 1962.

Hoffmeier, J. "The Memphis and Karnak Stelae of Amenhotep II (2.3)." In *The Context of Scripture. Volume II: Monumental Inscriptions from the Biblical World*, edited by W. Hallo and K. L. Younger, 19–23. Leiden: Brill, 2003.

Hornung, E. *The Ancient Egyptian Books of the Afterlife*. Translated by D. Lorton. London: Cornell University Press, 1999.

Huehnergard, J. "Remarks on the Classification of the Northwest Semitic Languages." In *The Balaam Text from Deir 'Alla Re-Evaluated: Proceedings of the International Symposium held at Leiden*, edited by J. Hoftijzer and G. van der Kooij, 282–93. Leiden: Brill, 1991.

Kennedy, T. M. "A Demographic Analysis of Late Bronze Age Canaan: Ancient Population Estimates and Insights through Archaeology." PhD diss., University of South Africa, 2013.

Lackenbacher, S. Ugaritica V no. 36. *Nouvelles assyriologiques brèves et utilitaires* 3 (1994) 51.

Lawler, A. "Uncovering Sidon's Long Life." *Archaeology* 64.4 (2012) 46–50.

Lemaire, A. "'House of David' Restored in Moabite Inscription." *Biblical Archaeology Review* 20.3 (1994) 30–37.

Lepsius, C. R. *Denkmäler aus Aegypten und Aethiopien*. Ergänzungband [Giza plates only]. Berlin: Nicolaische Buchhandlung. Leipzig: Hinrichs'sche, 1913.

Lichtheim, M. "The Poetical Stela of Merneptah (Israel Stela)." In *Ancient Egyptian Literature Volume II: The New Kingdom*, 73–77. Berkeley: University of California Press, 1976.

Massa, A. *The Phoenicians*. Translated by D. Macrae. Geneva: Minerva, 1977.

Mazar, A. *Archaeology of the Land of the Bible, 10,000–586 BCE*. Anchor Bible Reference Library. New York: Doubleday, 1990.

———. "The Egyptian Garrison Town of Beth-Shean." In *Egypt, Canaan, and Israel: History, Imperialism, Ideology, and Literature*, edited by S. Bar, D. Kahn, and J. J. Shirley, 155–89. Culture and History of the Ancient Near East 52. Leiden: Brill, 2011.

———. "The Search for David and Solomon: An Archaeological Perspective." In *The Quest for the Historical Israel: Debating Archaeology and History of Early Israel. Invited Lectures Delivered at the Sixth Biennial Colloquium of the International Institute for Secular Humanistic Judaism, Detroit, October 2005 by Israel Finkelstein and Amihai Mazar*, edited by I. Finkelstein and A. Mazar, 117–39. Archaeology and Biblical Studies 17. Atlanta: Society of Biblical Literature. Leiden: Brill, 2007.

———. "Temples of the Middle and Late Bronze Ages and the Iron Age." In *The Architecture of Ancient Israel from the Prehistoric to the Persian Periods: In Memory of Immanuel (Munya) Dunayevsky*, edited by H. Katzenstein, A. Kempinski, and R. Reich, 161–90. Jerusalem: Israel Exploration Society, 1992.

Mieroop, M., van de. *A History of the Ancient Near East*. Oxford: Blackwell, 2007.

Millard, A. R. "Assyrian Involvement in Edom." In *Early Edom and Moab*, edited by P. Bienkowski, 35–39. Sheffield Archaeological Monographs 7. Sheffield, UK: Collis, 1992.

Miller, J. M., and J. H. Hayes. *A History of Ancient Israel and Judah.* Louisville: Westminster, 1986.

Moran, W. L. *The Amarna Letters.* Baltimore: Johns Hopkins University Press, 1992.

Moscati, S. *The Phoenicians.* Milan: Bompiani, 1988.

Na'aman, N. "Four Notes on the Size of Late Bronze Age Canaan." *Bulletin of the American Schools of Oriental Research* 313 (1999) 31–37.

Quinn, J. C., N. McLynn, R. M. Kerr, and D. Hadas. "Augustine's Canaanites." *Papers of the British School at Rome* 82 (2014) 175–97.

Rainey, A. F. "Who Is a Canaanite? A Review of the Textual Evidence." *Bulletin of the American Schools of Oriental Research* 304 (1996) 1–15.

Sanders, S. L. *The Invention of Hebrew.* Traditions. Urbana, IL: University of Illinois Press, 2009.

Singer, I. "Purple-Dyers in Lazpa." In *Anatolian Interfaces: Hittites, Greeks and their Neighbours. Proceedings of an International Conference on Cross-Cultural Interaction, September 17–19, 2004, Emory University, Atlanta, GA,* edited by B. J. Collins, M. R. Bachvarova, and I. C. Rutherford, 21–43. Oxford: Oxbow, 2008.

Smith, S. *The Statue of Idri-mi.* Occasional Publications of the British Institute of Archaeology in Ankara 1. London: British Institute of Archaeology at Ankara, 1949.

Sparks, R. "Canaan in Egypt: Archaeological Evidence for a Social Phenomenon." In *Invention and Innovation. The Social Context of Technological Change 2: Egypt, the Aegean and the Near East, 1650–1150 BC,* edited by J. Bourriau and J. Phillips, 25–54. Oxford: Oxbow, 2004.

Stager, L. E. "The Impact of the Sea Peoples in Canaan (1185–1050 BCE)." In *The Archaeology of Society in the Holy Land,* edited by T. E. Levy, 332–48. Leicester, UK: Leicester University Press, 1995.

Stern, E. *Archaeology of the Land of the Bible 2, 732–332 BCE.* Anchor Bible Reference Library. New York: Doubleday, 2001.

Tubb, J. N. *Canaanites.* Peoples of the Past Series. Norman, OK: University of Oklahoma Press, 1998.

Tyson, C. W. *The Ammonites: Elites, Empires, and Sociopolitical Change (1000–500 BCE).* Library of Hebrew Bible/Old Testament Studies 585. London: Bloomsbury T. & T. Clark, 2015.

Vanderhooft, D. S. "The Edomite Dialect and Script: A Review of the Evidence." In *You Shall not Abhor an Edomite for He is Your*

Brother. Edom and Seir in History and Tradition, edited by D. V. Edelman, 137–57. Archaeology and Biblical Studies. Atlanta: Scholars, 1995.

Weippert, M. "The Israelite 'Conquest' and the Evidence from Transjordan." In *Symposia Celebrating the Seventy-Fifth Anniversary of the founding of the American Schools of Oriental Research (1900–1975),* edited by F. M. Cross, 15–34. Cambridge, MA: American Schools of Oriental Research, 1978.

Weiss, H. "The Northern Levant during the Intermediate Bronze Age." In *The Oxford Handbook of the Archaeology of the Levant c. 8000–332 BCE,* edited by M. L. Steiner and A. E. Killebrew, 367–87. Oxford: Oxford University Press, 2014.

Wente, E. F. *Letters from Ancient Egypt,* edited by E. Meltzer. Society of Biblical Literature: Writings from the Ancient World. Atlanta: Scholars, 1990.

Wightman, G. J. *Sacred Spaces: Religious Architecture in the Ancient World.* Ancient Near Eastern Studies 22. Leuven: Peeters, 2007.

Wiseman, D. J. *The Alalaḫ Tablets.* London: British Institute of Archaeology at Ankara, 1953.

Yasur-Landau, A. *The Philistines and Aegean Migration at the End of the Late Bronze Age.* Cambridge: Cambridge University Press, 2010.

Printed in the USA
CPSIA information can be obtained
at www.ICGtesting.com
LVHW021916101123
763491LV00001B/1